LIBERATING
SCHOLARLY WRITING

The Power of Personal Narrative

LIBERATING SCHOLARLY WRITING

The Power of Personal Narrative

ROBERT J. NASH

Foreword by Carol Witherell

Teachers College, Columbia University
New York and London

Publishers by Teachers College Press, 1234 Amsterdam Avenue, New York, NY 10027

Library of Congress Cataloging-in-Publication Data

Nash, Robert J.
  Liberating scholarly writing : the power of personal narrative / Robert J. Nash ; foreword by Carol Witherell.
       p. cm.
    Includes bibliographical references and index.
    ISBN 0-8077-4526-X (cloth : alk. paper)—ISBN 0-8077-4525-1 (pbk. : alk. paper)
       1. English language—Rhetoric—Study and teaching.
  2. Academic writing—Study and teaching.   3. Autobiography—Authorship.   I. Title.
  PE1404.N38   2004
  808′.042′0711—dc22   2004042282

ISBN 0-8077-4525-1 (paper)
ISBN 0-8077-4526-X (cloth)

Printed on acid-free paper
Manufactured in the United States of America

11   10   09   8   7   6   5   4   3   2

Contents

Foreword

"We teach who we are," Parker Palmer reminds us. Throughout my work as a teacher, scholar, and teacher educator, I have found this to be true. *Liberating Scholarly Writing* stands to have a profound and radical impact on educators, educational researchers, and professionals in counseling and human services. Writing from his experience as a teacher in an urban school and a professor of 35 years at the University of Vermont, Nash offers an engaging personal narrative as an educator who has lived by Palmer's principle. After reading this lively narrative of the life of a gifted teacher and scholar, which includes excerpts from his students' personal narratives, I find myself enlarging Palmer's statement: "We teach and learn who we are and who we might become." Isn't this duality of teaching and learning, of being and becoming, at the heart of all teaching and learning?

I loved reading this book. Nash considers his purpose to be one of gathering and reflecting on the meaning of his life as a teacher, learner, writer, philosopher, husband, and father. And so, as you might imagine, this is a courageous and profoundly honest book. Following in the narrative tradition of such scholars such as Ruth Behar, Jerome Bruner, Kieran Egan, Madeleine Grumet, Richard Rorty, and Jane Tompkins, Nash has offered a compelling intellectual and philosophical case for the importance of personal scholarly narrative in academic research and writing. He fully realizes his intent to pose autobiographical narrative as a "counter-narrative" to the faceless, de-contextualized research paradigm that has dominated scholarship in the professional schools for much of the past century. This is an important contribution to our intellectual life at a time when education seems to have lost its way, from the regressive move of K–12 education toward the kind of standardized instruction and testing so characteristic of the 1950s to the isolated disciplinary silos typical of much of higher education today. Both regressions are driven by fear; both need to be transformed into the pursuit of meaning, under-

standing, reflection, and inquiry that will guide our ethical, compassionate uses of our knowledge and skills. What better vehicle for such transformation than narrative?

Here's the paradox and the gift of this work: Even as Nash offers
cogent examples of scholarly personal narrative (or SPN) as a form of
scholarly research that is a radical departure from more traditional research designs, he skillfully grounds this approach in methods and truth
criteria that draw substantially from social science, science, philosophy,
and the humanities, all. Locating himself within the constructivist and
postmodern intellectual tradition, Nash explores through his own and
his students' personal narratives the ways that autobiographical writing
and story-telling can reveal the meaning that resides *and is taking new
shape* inside us, as well as among us as teachers and learners.

Whether reflecting on literature, a classroom event, a research venture, an event in our personal lives, or the tumultuous world we find
ourselves in today, we evoke, compose, and live the stories that shape
our personal and professional lives and give us meaning. I have long felt
that teachers who have this capacity for self-reflection, and who can pass
it along to their students through authentic personal narrative within
the subjects that they teach, extend a gift of great value. Truly excellent
teaching—in any subject, at any level—requires that we be fully present
to our students in an inquiring and reflective sense, even as we each
strive to make sense of the content before us and of our shaping of our
world. The sense-making will come from our ideas, our questions, our
creative work, and our shared passion for truth and meaning.

Nash's scholarly personal narrative and those of his students have
touched my life as a teacher, a scholar, a writer, an aspiring (and largely
self-taught) philosopher, and someone who has always been seized by
questions about other people and about the world we live in.

No "one-inch picture frame," this work. Rather, *Liberating Scholarly
Writing* offers a panoramic view of one teacher's journey, documented
in the richest of narratives from his own and his students' lives and
work. It's a monumental undertaking, so honestly offered, and of great
importance for professionals in education and human services and for
those who educate them—for those who seek to understand the power
of narrative in teaching and learning and in unleashing all that we might
become.

Carol Witherell, Professor of Education
Lewis & Clark College, Portland, Oregon
May 2004

Acknowledgments

My gratitude to all my students who have taken my Scholarly Personal Narrative (SPN) Writing Seminar is incalculable. I do not say this in any pro forma way. Without them, I just could not have written this book, period. Although I accept full responsibility for everything that I say here, my reason for even thinking about constructing such a text is due exclusively to the inspiration and challenges of my SPN students over the last half-dozen years. Moreover, I am secure enough to acknowledge that many of these students have been far more skilled SPN writers than I. I have learned much from these special, gifted writers, as well as from all the others who, like me, struggled patiently, sometimes despairingly, to construct narratives that were honest, self-disclosing, and scholarly, all at the same time.

I especially want to thank the following students for their permission to include extensive samples of their writing in this book: Dave Amsden, Patti Cook, Pamela Gardner, Joe Gervais, Tina Green, Kelly Johnson, Lou Lafasciano, David Moore, and Doug Walker.

I also want to express my profound appreciation to the following faculty at my university for their continuing, strong support of SPN scholarship in a professional school: Judith Aiken, Linda Backus, Penny Bishop, Judy Cohen, Rebecca Gajda, Deb Hunter, Bridget Turner Kelly, Cindy Gerstl-Pepin, Ray Proulx, Jen Prue, Betty Rambur, Peg Boyle Single, and Nancy Welch. Even though all but the last faculty member is a qualitative or quantitative scholar, each of them has kept an open mind and heart concerning the worth of SPN scholarship; but, more than this, each has kept me going during the rough times when I was trying to develop this controversial scholarly research approach for a professional school.

I continue to value the personal encouragement of scholars from other universities, including Kathleen Knight Abowitz, Jeni Hart, Michele Moses, Ernie Nalette, Ray Quirolgico, Jonas Soltis, Carney Strange,

Mike Waggoner, and Carol Witherell. Each of these scholars has carefully read the manuscript, offered their generous support, and made many excellent suggestions for improvement. I am indebted to all of them beyond words.

I wish to thank Carol Witherell for her gracious foreword and for her extraordinarily perceptive reading of my book when it was out for review. It should go without saying, but it won't, that I continue to be eternally grateful to Teachers College Press (TCP), and particularly to my editor, Susan Liddicoat, for publishing this, my fourth TCP book. TCP is one of the most prestigious educational presses in the world, and for them to take a chance with a book touting a very different type of professional research is encouraging, to say the least.

Finally, to Maddie, my partner of 45 years, I can only say thank-you for all that you've given me. You've enriched and deepened my own personal and professional narratives in ways that are simply too innumerable to mention. I'm pleased that you were able to take one of my graduate courses in SPN writing. You experienced firsthand the highs and lows of attempting to do this kind of boundary-crossing, personal scholarship. And your ongoing generous and constructive feedback has been invaluable in helping me to improve my conceptualization and teaching of SPN.

LIBERATING SCHOLARLY WRITING

The Power of Personal Narrative

CHAPTER ONE

Personal Narrative Writing Matters

If the goal of a dissertation [or thesis] is to produce the best piece of original scholarship a student is capable of, in a manner appropriate to one's field, then personal narrative should not only be acceptable but desirable. Allowing graduate students the full range of written expression should [be the goal of educators] who understand the importance of ethos and who should not exclude a whole mode of communication, especially a mode that enables a writer to both establish and question the authority of her experience. I am not a disinterested observer; why should I pretend to be? It is a matter of academic honesty.

—Tonya M. Stremlau, "The Personal Narrative
in Dissertation Writing: A Matter of Academic Honesty"

So for me it is no longer personal to be personal—it is fundamental. Once I include myself in the "audience" my contribution changes: my words lose their hortatory status, and take on instead the role of invitation, contribution, membership, and studenthood. I am no longer bound to argue, to make points and cases, or to think that whoever reads my work must be persuaded.

—David Bleich, "Recognizing the Human
in the Humanities"

I have been a college professor for over three-and-a-half decades in a professional school. If I had to guess, I'd say that I've read tens of thousands of students' papers since I first started teaching in higher education in 1968. Truth be told, and not wanting to offend anyone, I remember almost nothing of what I've read, unless the work was done in the last few years; or, more honestly, in the last few months. I admit that my amnesia regarding student-written papers may be a function of my age.

Yet here's the vital exception: I do tend to remember the scholarly writing of my students that combines both narrative and personal elements. Did I just say that I *remember* it? This is too weak. I meant that I *thrive* on it. I can't imagine *not* reading personal narrative writing at this particular time in my career.

I believe that students also fondly remember being able to write these types of papers. In fact, today, many graduates who have been out of school for several years will tell me they are able to recall these papers, almost page for page, years after they wrote them. One of the reasons they can do this with such vivid recall, I believe, is that they were given so few opportunities to write in the first-person voice; therefore, this type of project stands out even now. I have heard this particularly from people of color who have had to suppress their strong, distinct voices, along with their anger, for years in the academy. Another reason these personal papers are memorable, students have told me, is that these were the manuscripts they most enjoyed writing because they required a lot more creativity and candor than the usual research paper or literature review. Ironically, these creative papers were the ones that also pushed them the hardest.

Why, you might ask, is personal narrative writing important to educators and other helping professionals? This question is actually the impetus for the entire book that follows. But at this very early point, I will offer the following few thoughts. Good teaching, good helping, and good leadership are, in one sense, all about storytelling and story-evoking. It is in the mutual exchange of stories that professionals and scholars are able to meet clients and students where they actually live their lives. It is in the mutual sharing of our personal stories, particularly in the willingness of professionals to listen to the stories of others, that we make the deepest connections with those we are serving. It is in our stories that we, as professionals, and they, as students, can actually profess what we believe and hear what others profess to believe. Our stories get us closer to knowing who we are and who they are. Our stories are symbols for God, ethics, morality, justice, wisdom, truth, love, hope, trust, suffering and, most of all, what constitutes personal and professional meaning for all of us.

From both a personal and a professional standpoint, I have found that personal narrative writing helps us all to understand our histories, shape our destinies, develop our moral imaginations, and give us something truly worth living and dying for. Certainly, our students want competence, fairness, compassion, intellectual stimulation, and enthusiasm from us as educators. In my own opinion, though, they want something else equally as important. They want to be understood, and to be heard, from the nucleus of the stories they are living. They want to make a claim for some unchartered time to engage in honest, heartfelt narrative dialogue with us and with one another. Writing personal narratives in a scholarly setting is one way to achieve this desire. When done in an intellectually and emotionally respectable way, personal narrative writing can result in stunning self-insights. And I am here to testify, after spending over 35 years in the academy, that these are the learnings that stay with students, and with educators like myself, for the longest time.

I'm writing this book at this late stage in my career because I believe it's time for faculty to begin encouraging students to do more of this type of writing in schools of education and other professional units. Because I'm convinced that radical introspection and storytelling in scholarly writing have both particular (offering value for the storyteller) and universalizable (offering value for others) possibilities for professionals, I've arrived at a place in my own teaching where I want my students to "experience the full range of written expression" that Stremlau mentions in the epigraph to this chapter. I am convinced that all kinds of writing— personal narrative writing in particular—can reach, and even surpass, a professional school's highest scholarly standards. In some disciplines outside of education, it already has.

Moreover, I want faculty to value personal written expression to the extent that, if students choose to do this kind of writing (and a growing number wants to), it will be an acceptable (and respectable) genre for conducting certain kinds of research. I also want students to feel that personal writing matters to the academy, particularly to colleges of education, as much as any other kind of writing, especially when it's done well. And, I want them to believe that, in principle, it can be as "rigorous" (not "rigid," as in rigor mortis), and as scholarly, as any other type of research. All of this, to me, is what academic honesty and integrity are about.

Thus, I have in mind three types of audiences for this book:

- Degree-seeking undergraduate and graduate students who come from a number of venues in education and in the human services. Within this audience, I am especially interested in appealing to those students who self-identify as "other." These are minority students who have been traditionally underrepresented, marginalized, and disenfranchised in higher education, particularly in professional schools. Rarely do these students get an opportunity to tell their personal stories in formal scholarly writing assignments, or to challenge and question the dominant white, male, Western research ethos in the university. In fact, rarely do *any* of my students, white or otherwise, particularly in the sciences and social sciences, get a chance to enrich and deepen their scholarly activities with their personal perspectives.

- Graduate students in schools of education and other professional schools who are considering writing *theses and dissertations* using personal narrative methodology. This audience is particularly important to me, as you will see throughout my book.
- Faculty, researchers, and scholars in schools of education, and in other professional schools as well.

Please understand that I do not want to replace or undermine the more conventional research models in professional schools. How would this ever be possible or desirable? Every research paradigm in the academy—whether grounded in the traditional scientific method or in critical theory, in phenomenology or in hermeneutics, in ethnography or in statistics—has a valuable function to perform. Much good has come from all forms of university research through the decades. I personally value each and every method of scholarly inquiry, and I have borrowed generously from several approaches for my own research throughout my career.

In fact, the subtitle for this book could easily have been *Crossing Scholarly Genres*. Also, as a personal aside, one of my two daughters wrote a quantitative dissertation at Arizona State University; the other did a qualitative dissertation at the University of Vermont. I was present at both their dissertation defenses, and I cheered them on with my usual enthusiasm. These research modalities provided a perfect fit for the kind of dissertations they wished to write. I was happy for them, and grateful they were able to find methodologies compatible with their scholarly interests.

Rather than do an extended critique of the traditional research paradigms, then, what I want to do in this book is to argue for the validity of an alternative form of intellectual inquiry, what I will call *scholarly personal narrative* (I will refer to this as "SPN" throughout the book). For many reasons, some of which I will examine in the pages ahead, researchers in schools of education have grave doubts about the rigor of SPN scholarship. Some have called it soft. Others think it touchy-feely. Still others describe it as easy. A few think it is anti-intellectual. Some question its reliability and validity. These stereotypes are unfortunate. Why is it, students sometimes ask me, that when research departs from the older scientific-empirical models, it is automatically open to suspicion in the academy, especially in the professional schools? The answer is multidimensional, and I will be exploring some of these complexities in subsequent chapters.

I hope to make the case that SPN research is important in its own right, according to its own lights. SPN scholarship is controversial, at least in part, because it dares to redefine the idea of "rigor" to fit its own set of truth criteria. Some examples of these criteria are trustworthiness, honesty, plausibility, situatedness, interpretive self-consciousness, introspectiveness/self-reflection, and universalizability. Jerome Bruner adds the following truth criteria to what he calls "autobiographical narratives": coherence, livability, and adequacy.[1]

Actually, the social sciences and sciences have been redefining their own truth criteria in this direction for centuries in order to update and strengthen their own claims to universalizability, reliability, and validity.[2] SPN scholars, however, ask a series of personal, narrative-grounded, contextual questions that are too often ignored by researchers who use the more established frameworks. This major departure from the usual research norms in professional preparation programs doesn't make SPN scholarship better or worse, of course; it just makes it different. And difference can be threatening to many scholars who have been trained in the mindset that one research paradigm must fit all.

I often say to students that, from my postmodern perspective, difference in a research approach is good. It is especially good if it is pliable, fluid, and adaptable. It is good if it produces tangible benefits for others. It is good if it is personally honest and revealing, engaging, and probing. It is good if it is made accessible to everyone, particularly the nonspecialist. It is good if it is directed to the satisfaction of human needs, either for the near or for the far term. It can also be good for its own sake, particularly when it serves to enlighten, entertain, or inspire. Most important, I believe it is good if it is willing to continually examine and critique its own basic assumptions about what counts as defensible truth, knowledge, and value. A major aspect of my argument in this book will be that not all research needs to be replicable, validated, testable, or measurable in the same scientific ways in order to meet scholarly criteria. But more on this later.

In summary, my reasons for writing this book are as follows:

First, I intend to make a philosophical and pedagogical case for the worth of scholarly personal narrative writing in professional training programs. I will try to do this with humility. I will also work hard to avoid setting up straw men, whereby my view of what constitutes an alternative scholarship approach deteriorates into an angry polemic aimed at both real and imaginary enemies of SPN.

Having said this, however, I will mount a strong argument in behalf of the intellectual significance of SPN research in professional education programs. To do this with integrity, at times I will have to point out the many obstacles to realizing such an idealistic project. This means that, whenever necessary, I will be posing SPN as a counternarrative to the dominant research and scholarship narratives in professional schools. I hope to do this with generosity, but also with élan.

Second, I will offer a number of concrete, practical tips for those readers who might be interested in writing an SPN for a thesis or dissertation, publishable article, or book. Thus, I will be drawing generously from the work of many of my students during the last several years who have successfully gone on to do these types of writing projects. Their wise words will appear often in these pages. I only hope that I can do full justice to their insights without misinterpreting, or unwittingly exploiting, their hard-won achievements.

Third, despite what I said immediately above, I do not intend my book to be simply a technical writer's manual. Toward this more limited objective, I will cite a number of very good, how-to writing texts along the way and, also, in my "Recommended Books on Writing" section at the end of this text.[3] I will also offer my own practical tips about putting together an SPN, based on years of experience working with students at all levels in the academy.

What I mostly have in mind in writing this book, though, is to offer, you, my readers, an extended reflection on writing, teaching, learning, and living a fulfilled life as a professional *and* as a person. After all, I am a philosopher of education before I am a writing teacher. If I am skilled enough, and the reader is motivated enough, you will discover in this book many personal and professional rewards, not the least of which will be for you to be able to develop a philosophy of writing, a philosophy of education, and a philosophy of life, that just might coincide. I will actually encourage you to write about ideas by using the first-person "I" instead of relying exclusively on the third-person "he," "she," "it," or "they." I do not consider the first- and third-person voices, however, to be mutually exclusive in writing an SPN.

Fourth, I will try to accomplish something that I must, in all honesty, admit is dangerous: I will attempt to write about scholarly personal narrative writing by writing in a scholarly personal narrative style. In other words, I will include many personal stories about myself and my students, and other protagonists in my life as well, as a method for modeling the kind of scholarship I am recommending for professional programs in the university. Also, stylistically, I will mix much informal writing with formal writing.

Furthermore, I will try to use scholarly background references only when they are directly applicable. I will not pad my writing with an overflow of gratuitous attributions in order to prove that I have read every single last text on the subject of writing. I haven't. But who has? Also, I will place my references in a series of endnotes, so that they don't break up the aesthetic and logical flow of the chapter, as standard APA referencing tends to do. I find MLA or University of Chicago referencing formats to be more user-friendly for SPN writers. In particular, *The Chicago Manual of Style*, which I will follow in this book, allows for additional commentary on ideas which may not be central to the points I make in the text itself, but are important nonetheless.

I earlier described my planned SPN style of writing about writing as "dangerous," because my personal "I" approach risks distracting the reader from many important conceptual and technical points I wish to make. It also skates on the thin ice of authorial self-indulgence, a real turnoff for some readers. But the risk, in my mind, is worth it. These dangers, after all, are precisely what scholarly personal narrative writing at its best tries self-consciously to address and to resolve.

Fifth, I will interlace throughout my text references to a number of highly relevant, external sources, both philosophical and methodological, that I, and my students, have found to be useful in constructing SPN projects over the years. (Every once in a while I will mention a source that, in my opinion, seems to be unhelpful for constructing effective SPNs.[4]) At times I will let the authors of all of these relevant texts speak their own words. At other times, I will paraphrase and interpret them in my own language, and out of my own narrative take on what I think is good living, writing, and teaching. My biases will always be apparent to the reader, because I will make sure that they are upfront and clear at all times.

Sixth, I readily admit that I operate out of a postmodern perspective on the world. For the purposes of this book, I follow Richard Rorty's pithy summing up of postmodernism: truth is made, not discovered. This is to say that reality, while certainly existing "out there," is always and everywhere socially and personally constructed. Moreover, the best way to make sense of the "truth" of what is "out there" is through the construction, and telling, of stories, both to ourselves and to others. We impose stories on the world in order to tame it; in order to make manageable what William James called its "blooming, buzzing confusion"; or what one of my graduate students referred to as its "blur" that is nothing more than "one damned thing after another, and then we are old, and then we die, as does the universe." The latter two depictions of the world are the narrative depictions that make most sense to their respective authors. I, myself, prefer William James's take. He was about my age when he said this.

Thus, whenever I refer to the "real world" in my work, I do not mean the scientific world. My real world is not the world that can be empirically tested, measured, interviewed, weighed, or taxonomized, even though I am the first to admit that this story of the world can be of great value to scholars and researchers. Instead, I am speaking of the real world that each one of us narrativizes, the storied world that each one of us inhabits. Peter Ives says it well: "We do not write about things as they are or were or will be. We write about these things as *we* are."[5] Who are *we*, then? We are storied selves who write our own realities based on these unique stories.

I also acknowledge that I come at my writing and teaching as a moral philosopher, educational philosopher, literary theorist, and religious studies scholar. I have studied, taught, and written about these disciplines for the better part of four decades. Nevertheless, I promise that I will go out of my way, as best I can, to write a book that nonspecialist readers can both understand and enjoy. My purpose is not to obscure meanings in order to impress readers with the size of my specialized vocabularies and the extent of my background knowledge. I have been there and done that too many times for me not to be embarrassed whenever I reread some of my more obvious "academic showoff" writings.

Too frequently in my teaching and writing, I admit, I succumb to the temptation to be intellectually immodest. I am still working diligently on correcting this tragic flaw, even after I have been called on it by colleagues, loved ones, students, and friends for the better part of four decades in higher education. One of my daughters, a counseling psychologist at a university, calls this flaw my "narcissistic personality disorder." It is, in my opinion, the chief occupational hazard of the professoriate, particularly those who, like me, take ourselves, and our work, much too seriously.

One of the reasons that we take ourselves so seriously, I think, is that we have been trained to believe that scholarly writing must be impenetrable to the general public. Any other kind of writing is seen as pandering or, heaven forbid, "journalistic." I, for one, would be proud to be called a "public intellectual." This is someone who, in my mind, dares to bridge the specialized discourses between academicians and the lay public.[6] The public intellectual is a writer who is able to take a complex idea and communicate it in readable English, without compromising its integrity. In the very best sense of the term, SPN writers are "public intellectuals."

I am reminded here of something that an older, highly respected colleague once said to me decades ago when I first started teaching: "Robert, you'll find that the reason why intramural politics in the university can be so mean is that deep down we don't really think our work is very important in the eyes of the outside world. And so we cut each other to shreds in order to prove our own worth to ourselves."

I would only add to this bit of wisdom that I think too many of us adhere to the older, more established, argot-driven research and scholarly protocols and language systems, because deep down we are afraid to abandon, or even to reexamine, the ways in which we were trained to be respectable researchers and scholars. After all, the rewards for research conformity in the academy are many, including tenure, promotion, sabbaticals, grants, and that old standby—released time from teaching. In contrast, this book will present another evolving inquiry protocol that is no stranger to scholars in the humanities, but is still quite alien to professional schools.[7] In fact, this protocol has actually gotten professors tenured and promoted in such disciplines as philosophy, religious studies, literary theory, and feminist studies. My main objective will be to present this SPN protocol with clarity, simplicity, and spiritedness.

Whenever I feel that I must resort to using technical language to make my points, I promise that I will define what I mean in what I hope is accessible, down-to-earth English. But, some readers may rightfully ask: how do *you* know if *your* perception of down-to-earth English is the same as mine? Moreover, what is SPN anyway, and why is it so important to use down-to-earth English in writing it?

These are good, reasonable questions, and, at the end of the reading and writing day, only readers will be able to answer them for themselves. But the questions, and others like them, still need to be raised again and again. At their core, they are SPN questions that cry out for the telling of personal stories as a way to engage in the continual clarification of meanings. Even more, they entail on the reader's part a careful unpacking of these stories in order to discover, as near as possible, what writers actually mean by the languages they use and the stories they tell.

In a nutshell, SPN construction represents each writer's deliberate attempt to create a life by imposing a series of narrative-specific meanings on it. These meanings are always profoundly personal for each writer. Thus, writers must never take for granted the meaning of their own individual meanings for readers. Meanings in an SPN need to be unpacked again and again, through the telling of relevant stories and through the careful exposition, and extrapolation, of key ideas in those stories. What, for example, do I, Robert Nash, mean by "down-to-earth" language? Why am I even taking the trouble to write a book on SPN?

Why don't I capitulate to the research demands of the traditional university reward system, and, as one of my colleagues recently chided me, "just chill."

Why do I sometimes think of myself as a man on a mission? Is it possible for me to be on a mission without being a missionary? Why is this distinction important to me? In what ways have significant events and people in my life influenced my choice of what I think of as "down-to-earth" language, in order to tell my story of being a man on a mission? Is it possible that some of this inquiry might carry real meaning for my readers, most of whom will be educators and professionals in a variety of human services, including, primarily, teacher education and higher education leadership? How can I frame and compose my SPN story in such a way that it might have some generalizable appeal? By the way, in case you haven't noticed, we are already off and running in trying to make sense of SPN research. Stay tuned for much more.

A Brief Interlude:
Richard Rorty—A Philosopher on a Mission

The central pedagogical question that guides me as I write this book is a simple one: How can I describe SPN for my readers in such a way that it provokes, evokes, and invokes? I want to write a book that gets people thinking about scholarship in some fresh ways, that is provocative without being combative. I want to write a book that evokes from my readers the wish to tell their own stories, and possibly get them to try to find matches and mismatches between their stories and mine. Finally, I want to write a book that invokes, or calls upon, the stories of others, the stories of people who have come in and out of my life; as well as the stories of scholars and writers who have touched me in a special way. The invocation of conceptual and textual sources is, for me, the inescapable scholarly dimension of SPN writing.

In 1992, I stumbled upon an autobiographical essay written by one of my all-time philosophical heroes, Richard Rorty. I can honestly say that I have probably read in excess of a million words written by this author. It has been said about Rorty that he never had a thought he didn't publish. I believe that I have read most of them. I've assigned his books to my classes, referenced him in my own writings more than any other single author, and yearned to meet him in person. I never have. More than any other thinker, Rorty has shaped my own postmodern take on my life, profession, and world. But, sadly, he has always remained nothing more to me than a prodigious and prestigious scholar—a brilliant intellect devoid of any personal narrative that might have revealed his human qualities.

Then I read his essay "Trotsky and the Wild Orchids." I was moved beyond words. I read this short, 20-page essay five times on my first encounter with it. It completely enchanted me.[8] Rorty, for the first time in print, talks about his personal life. He makes himself vulnerable. For example, he confesses that it hurts him when people say that he merely "amuses himself" by "contradicting and attacking" others. When he was young, he hated being seen by his childhood acquaintances as a "clever, snotty, nerdy only child." The bullies sought him out and "regularly beat [him] up on the playground." He thinks often about his aching loneliness while he was growing up. He discusses the huge influence that his intellectual, atheistic, Communist parents had on his youth, particularly their unshakable commitment to social justice. He talks personally about his intellectual trajectory from wanting to be a Platonist while an undergraduate student at the University of Chicago, to becoming a Hegelian at Yale, to where he is today—a postmodern, Deweyian pragmatist, first at Virginia, and now at Stanford.

Time and time again in this autobiographical essay, Rorty, perhaps the most famous philosopher in the world today, expresses regret that "most people find his views repellent." He confesses in this very personal piece of writing that, contrary to his reputation, he is neither a political Marxist-Trotskyite nor a postmodern nihilist. He puts himself on record here as saying that his "politics are pretty much those of Hubert Humphrey." In fact, he finds "that the postmodernists are philosophically right though politically silly, and that the orthodox are philosophically wrong as well as politically dangerous." He goes on to admit that "I see the progressives as defining the only America I care about."

He also admits in plainspoken words something that he had been saying in very technical, philosophical terms for decades: "Philosophers are not the people to come to if you want confirmation that the things you love with all your heart are central to the structure of the universe, or that your sense of moral responsibility is rational and objective rather than just a result of how you were brought up." Rorty is acknowledging here that, as a philosopher, his wisdom, like our own, has serious limits. His is a humility sadly missing in the writings of most self-designated experts in the professions and scholarly disciplines.

He admits that if he had to do it all over again, he would become a poet or a novelist like Milan Kundera. For Rorty, the most that we can ever attain in a world where visions of certainty of one kind or another are infinitely contestable is simply a chance to tell others the religious or philosophical stories that engross us. Then we need to let people's unique tastes and temperaments take it from there. Poets and novelists do this far better than philosophers and politicians, according to Rorty.

I loved reading the above-mentioned personal essay. I admired Rorty's willingness to admit that, as a teenager, he often spent his days collecting up to 17 species of wild orchids in the mountains of northwest New Jersey. He uses this seemingly trivial snapshot of one slice of his private life to show that even he, the vaunted philosophical "relativist" and "historicist," was in need of some enduring truth that was "noble, pure, chaste . . . and morally superior" to everything else. The orchid embodied this purity for him. He also mentions, almost in passing, that the orchids more realistically represented a "sublimated sexuality" for him, because they were "notoriously sexy." Today, Rorty's orchid collecting has transmuted into bird watching. He is a globe-traveling bird-watcher of the first rank, willing to spend countless hours peering at rare birds through his binoculars.

Rorty's essay is an excellent example of an SPN that combines story and scholarship. It is both particular and general. It is concrete and abstract. It is down-to-earth and theoretical. It narrates fascinating elements of the author's personal story even while it elucidates his postmodern ideas in a fresh way. In fact, "captivating storyteller" and "insightful scholar" are the indivisible features of the same human being in this essay. Rorty's philosophical life recapitulates his personal life. His approach to doing philosophy is an inescapable by-product of the fascinating, multifaceted life he has led. Rorty's personal narrative makes crystal clear for the reader how he has managed to sustain a lifelong passion to make philosophical meaning.

If you want to understand how one world-renowned author is able to tell a very personal, reflective story of regret and triumph, in looking back at his life over a 45-year span as a philosopher, and yet not compromise one whit of the integrity of his scholarship, then read this essay. And, then, go on from there to find a way to do the same, but always in your own special style and according to the contingencies of your own story.

A Personal Confession

Before I close this chapter, I feel the need to make a very personal statement, in the best spirit of SPN writing. Therefore, I ask my readers to bear with me. If nothing else, my personal disclosure will give you some idea about the risks and benefits of personal narrative writing. Consider what I say below to be a sneak preview of what I think SPN is all about.

Consider it, also, the narrative context out of which I have written this book.

If you want to know where I, the author, am coming from with my various ideas and proposals, then what follows is essential information for you to have. If you really don't care who I am, and you would like to skip the rest of this chapter and move on to the more nuts-and-bolts stuff, or to the scholarly stuff, please feel free to do so. I understand fully. But I must warn you that I intend to interweave myself throughout this entire text. My personal presence will be obvious. After all, I am trying to write about SPN writing in an SPN style, so that my own practice might exemplify my theory.

I write what follows, then, in the form of a personal letter to each and every one of you:

Dear Readers,

It is important for you to know before we get started that I never expected to be a professor in a university. At most, I was resigned to remaining an English teacher in a large, blue-collar, urban public high school, where I spent three unhappy years. My social class background couldn't be more different from Richard Rorty's. I am the son of two working-class, blue-collar parents; one a Boston Irish cop, the other a stay-at-home, matriarchal mom. Both were orphans, and both had very little formal education. Both were also apolitical, unlike Rorty's openly Marxist parents; but, like his parents, my mother and father were atheists, albeit nonmilitant and unobtrusive ones. (They believed in angels but not in a God. Go figure.)

I was not an only child, nor was I "WASPY, nerdy, and snotty" like Rorty. I was one of five rough-and-tumble Irish brothers. In the birth order, I became the oldest after the tragic death of a firstborn. Thus, much was expected of me, and little was forgiven. After all, I had arrived on the scene as a kind of cosmic compensation for the untimely death of my parents' long-awaited firstborn son, Danny. In a sense, I was both Danny and Robert. In fact I still am, six decades later. There's a part of me that still thinks of myself as "Dan-ert."

Through public school, I was a very verbal, macho athlete who actually did as little reading and studying as possible, although I loved to draw and write. Rorty was a high intellectual achiever and genius, it appears, even before adolescence. He loved flowers. I can't remember ever seeing a single flower or plant in my home when I was young; in fact, in those days, I wouldn't have even been able to spell the word "orchid," let alone know that it was a flower with "sexy" connotations. The only birds I could identify right up to high school were pigeons.

Today, I am less Rorty's bird-watcher, and more the watcher of commercial films that crash, blow up, and blare, ESPN and Fox news, and professional athletic teams. I am transparently lowbrow in my aesthetic tastes, while Rorty is highbrow. In my politics, I am vaguely liberal, while Rorty is a passionate, old-fashioned, progressive populist. I do belong to the ACLU.

My formal education is first-generation, state college, not old-world wealth, Ivy League. I've scratched for everything I've ever gotten in the world. I went from a mediocre public school education to earn five degrees at various universities. Like Rorty, though, I've always been philosophical. Unlike him, I am an applied philosopher. I prefer teaching in a professional school rather than in a humanities department. I always wanted to work directly with practitioners, particularly educators and social service professionals.

Rorty and I share an interdisciplinary penchant. We like to shake things up in the academy. I can be intellectually provocative like Rorty, and I know that I've terminally irritated at least as many colleagues and students as he has. I suspect that my ego is as huge as Rorty's, but with far less justification. For one, I am no MacArthur Genius Award winner. My soaring ego notwithstanding, for decades I have been plagued by a miserable anxiety over whether I even belong in the academy. I don't sense that Rorty has ever had a single doubt about his august place in academia. This brings me up to the present time, when this year the poor, blue-collar, working-class narrative I too easily tell myself and others received a major jolt to its credibility. Or, in more accurate terms, my usual, self-serving, narrative spin got spun—in a very different direction.

When I learned recently that I was the 2003–2004 recipient of the University Scholar Award in the social sciences and the humanities, given by the "public Ivy" University of Vermont, I had many mixed feelings. Mind you, this is a much-sought-after honor granted annually to a faculty member who has compiled a record of "outstanding sustained research and scholarly contributions to both the academic discipline and the University of Vermont." Obviously, I was proud, and, truth to tell, feeling a little boastful, because I was only the third person to receive this prestigious award in the history of my professional unit, the College of Education and Social Services. I immediately thought: This must make me special, right? This validates my career, right? Isn't this what every professor wishes to achieve—the officially certified, intellectual respect of his peers?

Other thoughts struck me as well. Does this award mean that I can finally hold my own with all those imperious academicians from other units in the university who frequently look down their noses at education professors like me? Too many arts and sciences professors I know consider what I and my colleagues do in teacher education seminars, and in our research, to be trivial and anti-intellectual. To them, the thrust of our work lies somewhere between training nursery school teachers to change diapers and brainwashing public school teachers to make their students feel good, in spite of how much or how little these students actually achieve academically.

"Educationists," the intellectual rigorists will sometimes snarl, "don't belong in a university. What *they* do to further the self-esteem of students and coddle them is inferior, and what *we* do to further rigorous scholarship and in-depth knowledge of the disciplines is superior." Could I now look at these detractors and think smugly: *And when's the last time that you were named a University Scholar? My self-esteem is just fine, thank you. How's yours? Heh, heh.*

But, alas, this smugness of mine soon became short-lived, as other, conflicting feelings intruded. It didn't take long for me to think, *Just what the hell have I really done to merit the title of "University Scholar"*? Many colleagues in my own College of Education and Social Services (CESS) have been engaged for a long time in what social science rigorists usually think of as hard, empirical research. Most of my educationist colleagues are predisposed to weigh, measure, or interview in order to arrive at valid educational hypotheses and conclusions. Many of them do this extremely well, and a few have even achieved a level of national reputation that is striking.

Some of my colleagues are qualitative researchers; some quantitative. Some do field and laboratory studies; some do complex multivariate analyses. Some are policy analysts; some are policy makers. Some carry out their research in order to help public school teachers, administrators, and social service professionals transform their organizations in beneficial and practical ways. Some serve directly as advisors to the power brokers in schools, colleges, and social service agencies. What, I wonder, do *I* do that is worthwhile? I publish a lot, but so what? Others do as well.

What made me most sad, however, in thinking about my newly bestowed honor, was the fact that, all too often, my colleagues and I speak very different scholarly languages whenever we are discussing the value of thesis and dissertation research. We tend to talk past, through, over, and under one another. Furthermore, we see our own research and teaching missions in sometimes diametrically opposing ways. Our expectations for what constitutes sound scholarship, particularly at the graduate level, rarely mesh. More often than I care to admit, I am prone to give in to the temptations of a self-pitying paranoia. Or, worse, I have shameful daydreams of becoming an aggressor, whose mission is to destroy the shopworn, narrow research conventions of professional schools like mine.

What frustrates me most of the time though, is that, no matter how hard I try, I am unable to find the most effective reconciling languages, or the common points of contact in contrasting research stories, that might bridge the divide that separates me from others in my professional school. I want more than anything to be an intellectual peacemaker and an interdisciplinary collaborator. I want to be a colleague who finds "narrative overlap" in the work that we all do, no matter how different our approaches, in order to prepare students to be competent and caring educators and other human service professionals. In order for me to do this, of course, I need first to stop setting up self-defeating, me-versus-them dualisms. I'm learning to be less polemical.

But it's still damned hard to find many allies in my own college. As far as I know, I am the only faculty member in my professional college whose degrees, training, and intellectual predilections are all humanities-based. I say this, mind you, without a shred of arrogance or antagonism. In fact, I have often felt that I am an intellectual fish out of water in my professional school. I am a philosopher of education whose academic training is in philosophy, literary theory, ethics, religious studies, and educational theory. Most of the other fish in my college are trained in the social, natural, or professional sciences. I tend to think of education as a humanity; my colleagues think of it as a social science or a professional science.

And so my doubts and my self-pity get easily activated: Is my way of coming at the world of education and scholarship as valuable as theirs? Is what I do respected by them? Does the fact that I exist outside of what they would call the "dominant research paradigm" of professional schools of education and social services automatically marginalize me; or, in the testy word of one of my colleagues, am I forever destined to be an "outlier"? Why in the world does this matter so much to me?

I tend to speculate, question, and philosophize in my scholarship. My colleagues, in contrast, test, verify, and extrapolate. I look for hidden subtexts and pretexts *inside* assigned readings and inside colleagues' and students' assumptions about their lives and professions. My colleagues look for what is observable and verifiable in the world *outside* the text and beyond the individual psyche. I am more interested in what my students are able to narrate about their own lives in pursuit of the self-knowledge that often occurs from this type of intimate and honest, storytelling activity. My colleagues are more concerned with what students are able to demonstrate qualitatively or quantitatively by examining objective data. All of this is good, of course, if one or the other approach isn't pushed to an extreme, and if it doesn't crowd out those writers who might come at an understanding of research in an entirely different manner.

But alas, some students do get crowded out. My heart goes out to those scores of graduate students I have known over the years, who are about to begin the daunting task of getting in the right mindset for writing theses and dissertations. They often come to me with a common complaint: "I just can't get started. Where's the 'me' in all of this? Why can't I just write a dissertation that people, in addition to those on my defense committee, will want to read? Why do I have to write in the third person, passive voice? Why can't I show my passion and excitement for my topic in my own writing style without making it as dry as dust?

"Why is it that my thesis needs to be crammed with every scholarly reference under the sun, even when these are not directly related to my content? Why do I need to show off? Why must I continually suppress my own personal voice? Why do I have to continue to whittle away at my interests in search of a researchable topic for my dissertation; and, in the process, end up with something so overspecialized and trivial that it fails to appeal to anyone but a mere handful of readers? Can't I demonstrate that I know the literature in my field, that I possess the requisite analytical skills in my discipline, and that I can formulate and solve problems, without turning my work into one long literature review qua book report? Or into a lengthy statistical or qualitative analysis whereby the means of my research completely overwhelms my ends? Or into 200 pages of precise methodological explanation, all of which ends up sounding full of learned sound and fury, but which really signifies nothing of any lasting value?"

Many of my colleagues, of course, recognize the validity of these complaints, because they have either heard them or uttered them themselves at one time or another. Some of these colleagues, therefore, take justifiable pride in producing graduate students for the professions who are not merely disembodied research machines. Instead, they wish to produce social justice activists, or on-site consultants, or institutional change agents. These colleagues prefer what they call "action research."

This is a type of research that is less theoretical and philosophical than what I do, and not as personal, although it can be. Action research gets students involved firsthand in the communities that they are studying. At its best, action research results in beneficial changes at all levels of human service delivery systems. It also carries the promise of transforming a graduate student's life by fostering a genuine sense of personal agency and professional impact. At its worst, though, action research creates the impression that unless scholarship always leads to concrete, institutional changes, then, for professionals, it is beside the point—a mere bagatelle in the "practical" scheme of things.

To be fair, there are some scholars in my college, and throughout the country, who are experimenting with a variety of more personal forms of ethnographic research. Ruth Behar, for example, is doing what she calls "vulnerable anthropology" and "self-reflexive, shadow biography." (I talk more about Behar's work in Chapter 2.) Margaret Willard Traub reconstructs the "memoirs" of her field respondents against the backdrop of her own evolving "scholarly memoir." A former colleague of mine, Corinne Glesne, is doing "poetic transcription" and "autobiographical ethnography." Some scholars speak of using field studies as a way to produce "radical introspection," both in the subject being studied *and* in the researcher. Other anthropological investigators are doing "biographical ethnography" and "autoethnography." I appreciate these and similar initiatives to enlarge the more conventional, positivistic research modalities.[9] In my opinion, these initiatives are a necessary precondition for recognizing the unavoidable role that the ethnographer's *self* plays in interviewing, analyzing, and generalizing.

What I am advocating, however, takes qualitative research one major step further. SPN puts the *self* of the scholar front and center. The best SPN interview is the scholar's self-interrogation. The best analysis and prescription come out of the scholar's efforts to make narrative sense of personal experience. All else is commentary—significant, to be sure, but commentary nonetheless. The ultimate intellectual responsibility of the SPN scholar is to find a way to use the personal insights gained in order to draw larger conclusions for readers; possibly even to challenge and reconstruct older political or educational narratives, if this is an important goal for the reseacher.

During the 1990s, I rediscovered the work of Jerome Bruner, whose classic book *The Process of Education* changed the face of K–12 pedagogy throughout the United States decades ago. Bruner has since undergone what he calls a "narrative turn" in his thinking. Today, he says that in the social sciences "the truth that matters is not empirical truth but . . . the *narrative* truth." An empirical, cognitive psychologist for several decades, Bruner has since come to believe that the best way to understand the "self" is to think of the self as a storyteller, "a constructor of narratives about a life." In fact, for Bruner, there is no fixed, hidden entity that one calls a "self." Rather, the self is really a multiple telling of narratives. The self is a "distributed self, enmeshed in a net of others," whose primary task is to make meanings through narration.[10]

What exactly is Bruner saying here? If social scientists want to understand human behavior in all of its complexity, then Bruner is urging them to begin with the stories that people tell about themselves and about their involvement with others. According to Bruner, "self" is nothing more than a narrator's creative construction, not some incontrovertible essence that makes each one of us truly unique and special. "Self" is whatever story we construct about who we are, depending on whom we are with, and who we would like to be, at any given time. The best way to think about the "self," then, is as a storyteller who needs to narrate a number of stories in order to create meanings. If this is an accurate depiction of Bruner's latest thinking about the "self," then, by extension, ethnographic interviewers will need to learn new ways of coding people's stories. "Distributed," changing personal narratives do not fit conventional scientific categories.

I strongly recommend Jerome Bruner's wonderful book *Acts of Meaning* for educators and human service professionals. This book is Bruner's official rejection of a concept of mind as "information processor" in favor of a new concept: *mind as a creator of narrative meanings*. I find Bruner's work over the last decade to be a powerful affirmation of the intellectual value of SPN. Moreover, I am fast becoming a postmodern Brunerian, a designation that I am sure Jerome Bruner, the rigorous social scientist and winner of the International Balzan Prize, would consider incoherent. But this is okay. I admire his work nonetheless.

Some of my colleagues say that I am a constructivist in my approach to knowledge, and empirical researchers are objectivists or positivists. I'm not so sure, though, that this pat little dichotomy is tenable. In fact, it has always bothered me. According to philosophers, constructivists are people who approach the world as a phenomenon to be studied primarily from the inside out; objectivists approach the same phenomenon from the outside in. Constructivists tend to ask: What meaning lies *inside* of you, and how can you best narrate it? Objectivists ask: What meaning lies *outside* of you, and how can you best prove it? In reaction to this overly facile dichotomy, though, I would offer that, at some level, we are all constructivists *and* objectivists.

Scratch an empirical researcher, or a no-nonsense, just-the-facts teacher, or a positivist scientist deeply enough, and you will find a closeted constructivist, just waiting for permission (and legitimacy) to go public with some pretty fascinating personal stories and learnings. I would quickly add, however, that, at some level, we are all objectivists as well. Scratch a phenomenologist, or a memoirist, or a postmodernist deeply enough, and you will find a closeted objectivist, just waiting for the decisive empirical research that will ground and validate all the insights gained from narrating fascinating, personal stories and learnings.

You see, we, in the university, whether we like it or not, are of mixed intellectual temperaments to some extent or other. Some of us are more dominant in our constructivism, some more dominant in our objectivism. But none of us is ever completely free of the opposite, recessive perspective on the world; nor should we be, in my opinion. I am a dominant constructivist and a recessive objectivist in my teaching and scholarship. At times, I am both storyteller and story verifier; narrator and analyzer; values seeker and facts finder; inside the text and outside the text; humanist and social scientist. I suspect that this is what some of my fellow scholars in my own college and throughout the university find to be of value in my own scholarship. Maybe not.

I would not be at all surprised if the humanists and the scientists on the University Scholar Awards committee at my university went back and forth on the worth of what people like me do in our research and teaching. I know that I myself waver frequently on the measure of my true value to students, colleagues, and discipline. But after working in the academy for 36 years, having taught thousands of students ranging from 18 to 85 years of age, and after having published over 100 interdisciplinary articles and several books, I always end up at the same place. Should I, an "out" narrative constructivist in a professional school, continue to do what I have always done, and let the chips fall where they may? Or should I try to break some new intellectual ground before I retire, and allow my closeted objectivist leanings to come through in my teaching and writing? Please know, dear readers, that I am still working on finding that intellectual balance. It's definitely easier on some days than others.

Rest assured, however, that despite my neurotic self-doubts, I am here to tell you that I will not return the University Scholar Award anytime soon. There is still a part of me that wants to show my colleagues that what I teach and publish is important for all professional students to experience, even though many of them recognize this already. Also, maybe it's just that I am proud to be an outlier, a renegade of sorts. Perhaps this is the story that I choose to live within, and project without. It is entirely possible that, in my mind, this is the narrative that has helped me to survive as a fish-out-of-water, university professor for over 35 years. I have constructed myself through the years to be seen as the interdisciplinary border crosser in my professional school, the research iconoclast, the scholarly skeptic, the classroom teacher as postmodern provocateur.

So what does all of this mean for the book before you that you are about to read? I chose to tell you about this one recent incident in my personal story in the previous paragraphs because whatever I say in the pages ahead is always a reflection of the teaching and writing narratives that I have lived these many years in the academy. It is also a function of my temperament, philosophical training, and my worldview. What you will read in this book is the unavoidable product, the sum total, of my life's narrative. I write what I have lived. There is no other way.

The truth is that I, like most scholars I know, write mainly to explain myself to myself. I also write to explain myself to others. Moreover, I write with the passionate conviction that I have something unique and helpful to offer my students and colleagues in a professional training college. If I can win a prestigious honor for my work, so can you, if this is your need. If it isn't, I fully understand, and in some ways I envy you.

But, at the very least, let my personal story, along with its peculiar strengths and deficiencies, be the backdrop for what I want this book to achieve for all of you. More than anything, if you are ready for it; and if you are willing to work hard to achieve it; and if you have the temperament for it, you will be able to construct an SPN of which you, and the academy, can be proud. You will be composing your life in such a way that other lives will be touched, and maybe even enriched. Is there anything better than this for a scholar to accomplish?

In Conclusion

And, so, I am closing this chapter during the long days of a beautiful, lush green, Vermont summer. Outside my study, my wife works in the garden. My three young grandchildren play soccer, come inside my house at frequent intervals to forage for food in my pantry and refrigerator, and nag us to make those pleasurable trips to Rocky's ice cream stand around the corner to buy delicious, cool creamies.

My family is in the process of preparing for a week-long vacation trip to North Carolina to visit my youngest daughter, Kayj, and her husband, Brockett, who live near the ocean in Wilmington. I may or may not accompany them. If I run true to form, I will probably choose, instead, to remain at home to pound the keys of what is now a collector's item, my original G-4 Mac Cube computer, in a very messy, yet gloriously quiet, room, each and every day without fail. My study, you see, is my refuge, my getaway space. It is not a prison. How could it be? It is the place where I make meaning.

In spite of the clutter of books, papers, and "stickies" all around me, and in spite of all the mind-boggling little routines I need to follow each and every day in order to get to a mind-space where I can put my butt on a chair for several hours to type, I love every single minute of what I am doing. For one, writing, to my mind, is the single, supreme act of vanity and self-satisfaction that is actually admired by others, especially if it manages to get published. Acting may be another. In the academy, though, it is published scholarship that gets the professor rewarded with tenure and promotions, along with other desirable perquisites.

Both within and without the academy, a writing project promises to immortalize the writer like no other activity. It declares that what we have to say might actually be important to others. It outlives all the seasons, and all the summer vacations, and all the trips to other states and other countries and, yes, all the delicious creamies waiting to be devoured on hot summer days. It is the ultimate culmination of our human need to construct the stories that give order and meaning to our, and others,' lives.

To write is to demonstrate with a degree of certainty that we truly matter. Is it too extravagant to say, paraphrasing Descartes, that I write, therefore I exist? I don't think so. To write a personal narrative is to look deeply within ourselves for the meaning that just might, when done well, resonate with other lives; maybe even inspire them in some significant ways. Writing is the ultimate trip for an educator. It leaves an indelible mark on the universe, even if its only palpable achievement is to bring about one small, undramatic change in a school, home, neighborhood, social service agency, or in a single classroom. To write a creative personal narrative in a professional school so that it enlarges, rather than undermines, the conventional canons of scholarship is, in my opinion, to transform the academy and the world. May each of my readers discover this wonderful truth for themselves—in their own manner, in their own place, and in their own time.

CHAPTER TWO

What Is Scholarly Personal Narrative Writing?

A serious life, by definition, is a life one reflects on, a life one tries to make sense of and bear witness to. The age is characterized by a need to testify. Everywhere in the world women and men are rising up to tell their stories out of the now commonly held belief that one's own life signifies.

> —Vivian Gornick, *The Situation and the Story:*
> *The Art of Personal Narrative*

That voice coming at you contains a world. It's not merely telling you things, it's telling them in a way that reveals the habits of mind and quality of feeling that give your subject his uniqueness. That's all in there, wrapped in an idiolect of vocabulary and syntax and inflection. Getting the key to it gives you access to a mind. . . . Capture the personal voice and you've gone a long way toward capturing the person.

> —David Chanoff, "Guided by Voices:
> The Work of a Ghostwriter"

Validity is subjective rather than objective: the plausibility of the conclusion is what counts. And plausibility, to twist a cliché, lies in the ear of the beholder. Validity, in short is an interpretive concept, not an exercise in research design.

> —Lee Cronbach, *Designing Evaluations*
> *of Educational and Social Programs*

Your Own Life Signifies

Right away, let me give you the shorthand answer to the question that I ask in the title of this chapter. Scholarly personal narrative writing is the unabashed, up-front admission that your "own life signifies," in the words of Gornick, quoted above. That is to say that your own life has meaning, both for you and for others. Your own life tells a story (or a series of stories) that, when narrated well, can deliver to your readers those delicious aha! moments of self and social insight that are all too rare in more conventional forms of research.

The rest of this chapter, indeed the entire book, will be but an extended examination of my belief that there is genuine wisdom and meaning in the unique life you are creating for yourself and for others. Furthermore, I contend that what you have lived, loved, loathed, and learned in a lifetime of extraordinary (or ordinary) challenges and satisfactions can be of enormous benefit to others. This is predicated, of course, on my assumption that you are willing to take the risks to delve deeply into your lives and then go public with the results; and that you can narrate all of this with passion, intelligence, and compassion.

This is a tall order, I know, and SPN is not everyone's natural preference, nor should it be. But for those of my students who have done this kind of writing over the years, they have experienced SPN as a special gift. Among other things, it has bestowed on them the right to find and express their own, unique writer's-scholar's voice. If critics of SPN think that this discovery is inconsequential in the larger academic scheme of things, then I invite them to interview each and every single one of my SPN writers. They might be surprised at what they hear.

Hearing the Sound of Your Own Voice

Ralph Waldo Emerson once said that it is impossible to utter even two or three sentences without letting others know where you stand in life, what you believe, and which people are important to you. Voice in SPN writing is the unique tone and style of the author. It's the "you" whom you are choosing to tell your story. It's the recognition that you can never be fully outside your writing. As an author, you are always an insider; not omnisciently removed from what you write, but caught up personally in every word, sentence, and paragraph; in every statistic and every interview; in every comma and period. Your writing, at some point, will always give your personal story away, even when you attempt to cloud it with the thick idiom of academese and objectivity.

SPN is about giving yourself permission to express your own voice in your own language; your own take on your own story in your own inimitable manner. SPN is your grand opportunity to practice listening to the sound of your own voice. Find your special sound and style, and you will find your story. Lose these, and you will continue to be silenced. Writing will be impossible—if not now, then soon; and probably forever.

How important is *voice* to those literary and rhetoric scholars and professors who, having been trained in traditional models of objectivist scholarly writing, have actually begun writing in a personal narrative genre? "Listen" to the following, by Gil Haroian-Guerin:

> I discovered who I am, as an American, an Armenian, and a female, the granddaughter of certain women. The Armenians are a marked people. That's why I had to mark the page. I learned why I have to write.

Here is another response, this time by Ann E. Green:

> I spend a lot of time when I'm teaching and writing trying to remember where I am, where I come from. The question of where I am has a lot to do with who I am; my family likes to stay in one place and has, for the last one hundred and fifty years or so. So when I think about the stories that I write about my teaching, they are connected to place, to the literal politics of location that determine where students and I are, how I read their writing, and how they read me. I am a heterosexual white woman from what can sometimes be called a "working-class background."

Consider a comment by Maria-Cristina Kirklighter:

> I've been told that personal essays count for very little in enhancing my vitae. I've been told that critiquing academia through personal essays is risky business. In other words, I've finally been told that these words are to be divorced from my experiences if they are to hold academic ivory value. So here I sit as a disrobed, ivoryless, and Honduran/Southern Angla contemplating these conflicting values.... But I also know that the only avenue I have for reaching a non-Honduran/Southern Angla audience and making them see what some of these words mean to me is through the personal.

Deborah Mutnick reacts as follows:

> The personal narrative allows me to penetrate what often seems like a shield of impersonal, often jargon-ridden, formulaic prose, which we use at least in part to cover up our insecurities, and to contribute substantively to the construction of new knowledge about everyday life.

Finally, "hear" the words of Louise Wetherbee Phelps:

> Among other reasons, I write personally to dramatize the living mo-
> ment of thought and portray it as passionately felt; to make intellectual
> life and academic work intelligible as experience, embedded in and
> reflecting daily life and personal identity.[1]

What my SPN students all have in common, despite their many
differences, is the similar conviction expressed by the scholar-teachers
whom I quote above: Their lives truly matter. They signify. They are not
living in a vacuum but rather in a series of overlapping, concentric circles with others. They affect, and are affected by, the actions of others.
My SPN students are in the process of continually learning how best to
share their most cherished meanings with others in mutually respectful,
written exchanges.

Most important, though, my students believe deep down that they
have earned the right to put themselves into their scholarship. They
know that, whether critics of personal writing like it or not, writers are
always an integral part of what they observe, study, interpret, and assert.
The inclusion of the self in research and scholarship is inescapable, even
more so when writers try intentionally to excise the self from their research. The "I" voice always has a way of seeping into an "objective,"
third-person text. My students have learned to accept this subjective
seepage, indeed, even to celebrate it. I am pleased when they do.

But not all students are convinced of the worth of the personal voice
in their scholarship. A student once went public in my seminar with this
comment: "I don't see why it's necessary to dig so deeply into the mar-
row of my own life. Can't I find truth in the voice of others? Can't I talk
and write about *their* truths? After all, what is higher education for
unless it teaches us how to write by using the language and ideas of
experts?"

My answer went something like this: "Of course there is truth in the
voice of others, just as there is truth in your own voice. I can only say to
you that each one of us must someday explain and claim our truths in
our own voices. Long after you receive your degree, and long after you
have become the professional you have been trained to be, you will still
be left with something that never goes away. You will be left with that
craving to find out what's inside of you, what makes you more than
how you've been shaped by the academy to talk and write.

"By all means, write your dissertation in a way that demonstrates a
grasp of your discipline's specialized nomenclature and research methodology. But don't risk losing something vital and special to your hu-

manity: your own gritty and beautiful, hard-won voice. I don't really care where you find your wisdom. I just want to encourage you to express it, whenever and however you feel comfortable, out of the heart and soul of your own lived life."

Here is Anne Lamott, who is far more eloquent on the same point I am trying to make:

> But you can't get to truths by sitting in a field smiling beatifically, avoiding your anger and damage and grief. Your anger and damage and grief are the way to the truth. We don't have much truth to express unless we have gone into those rooms and closets and woods and abysses that we were told not to go in to. When we have gone in and looked around for a long while, just breathing and finally taking it in—then we will be able to speak *in our own voice* and to stay in the present moment. And that moment is home.[2]

Memoirs, Personal Narrative Essays, and Autobiographies

Let me continue my SPN commentary with another quotation posed by Vivian Gornick. She is speaking here of what she calls "memoir writing," which is synonymous with what I think of as personal narrative writing.

> A memoir is a work of sustained narrative prose controlled by an idea of the self under obligation to lift from the raw material of life a tale that will shape experience, transform events, deliver wisdom. Truth as a memoir is achieved when the reader comes to believe that the writer is working hard to engage with the experience at hand. What happened to the writer is not what matters; what matters is the large sense that the writer is able to make of what happened.[3]

Notice that, for Gornick, a memoir, like SPN, starts with the *writer's life* rather than with the lives and activities of others. It is up to the writer to make sense of the "raw material of life" by looking inward, not outward, at least initially. Notice, too, that the major truth criterion in personal narrative writing differs drastically from more empirically based forms of research and scholarship. Personal narrative writing is "true" when writers work hard to make personal meaning of the raw material of their day-to-day experiences in a way that readers believe it. I will talk more about what counts as validity and truth in SPN writing in the section following this one.

Moreover, it is not enough simply to tell a personal story that carries no explicitly intended meaning for readers. This type of self-contained,

confessional writing has its place, of course, and readers, myself included, have enjoyed its sundry pleasures for centuries. Think of St. Au-
gustine's, and, later, Jean Jacques Rousseau's, *Confessions*. Think, even
more up to date, of Mary McCarthy's *Memories of a Catholic Girlhood*,
Maxine Hong Kingston's *The Woman Warrior*, and James Carroll's *An
American Requiem: God, My Father, and the War That Came between Us*. But
Gornick, like all SPN writers, has additional purposes in mind.

Scholarly personal narrative writing is meant primarily to benefit
readers, touch readers' lives by informing their experiences, by transforming the meanings of events, and, in Gornick's telling phrase, by "delivering wisdom." All of this is the author's expressed outcome, not just
for the writer, but for the reader as well. Gornick punctuates this give-
and-take, this to-and-fro between the writer and the reader of personal
narrative, by saying that, in the end, what simply *happens* to the writer
is not what truly matters. What matters is the "large sense" of meaning
that the writer is able to convey both to self and to readers about what
simply happens.

In another place, Gornick distinguishes between a *personal narrative
essay* and a *memoir*. A *memoir* is what writers compose when they use
subject matter to explore their personal "personae." A personal narrative
essay reverses the focus. In this latter instance, writers use their personae
in order to explore subject matter other than themselves. For example,
Tina, one of my students, a white mother of four biracial children, who
decided to write an SPN *essay* for her master's thesis, used her own personal, negative experiences with predominantly white public schools as
as a pretext for looking more deeply into the pervasive existence of subtle acts of racism and bias in school curricula in her district. She called
her thesis *Maiming the Spirit: The Journey of Brown Children through White
Schools*.

She began by recounting her own, inward personal torment over
how much her children had suffered at the hands of racially oblivious
white administrators and teachers. She worked outward from there to
discover the larger implications for combating such ignorance in schools
and communities everywhere. Her thesis ended in a series of important
antiracist policy proposals that show promise of changing curricula and
classroom teaching at all levels of schooling in her district.

If she had been writing an SPN *memoir*, she would have shifted her
perspective and focus by using acts of institutionalized racism and bias
in public education in order to go inward to explore questions in her
own personal life. Why, for example, did she marry a black man, knowing that she risked terminal alienation from her working-class family
and friends? Why is it that she always manages to choose the difficult

path in life? Why hasn't anything really been easy for her as she attempts to live out her story as a wife, parent, educator, and graduate student? Who is she to think that she can be an antiracist who will actually make a difference in the lives of public school teachers and children? Who or what gives her the right to be a crusader? How can she do this antiracist work without turning into the kind of self-righteous zealot she herself detests?

Depending on the writer's intellectual purposes, scholarly personal narrative writing can include either memoirs or essays, as well as a number of other formats. For example, one scholar, Louise Z. Smith, talks about the advantages of "writing ourselves" in a series of letters to significant others in lives. She goes so far as to urge teachers to set up "epistolary symposia" in their seminars as a way of making closer personal contact with their students; and as a way to get them closer to the personal meaning of what they are reading and talking about with one another.[4] Margaret Gillett and Ann Beer argue that autobiographical narratives, either oral or written, can also be desirable forms of scholarship in the academy. Why? In their own words:

> These narratives are part of a change in thinking which at last acknowledges that the autobiographies of "ordinary" people can construct new knowledge about society. They can also challenge and reconstruct historical understanding in ways unthinkable even a generation ago.[5]

The point I am trying to make is that scholarly personal narrative writing can take many different forms. While it is personal, it is also social. While it is practical, it is also theoretical. While it is reflective, it is also public. While it is local, it is also political. While it narrates, it also proposes. While it is self-revealing, it also evokes self-examination from readers. Whatever its unique shape and style of communicating to readers, an SPN's central purpose is to make an impact on both writer and reader, on both the individual and the community. Its overall goal, in the words of David Bleich and Deborah H. Holdstein, is "to admit the full range of human experience into formal scholarly writing."[6]

By the way, personal narrative essays and memoirs sometimes contain an *autobiographical* component. I think of autobiographies as more chronological and linear in structure and format, more historical and episodic in focus, than essays and memoirs. I think of the latter two genres as offering a narrower lens on the writer's life, what Anne Lamott calls a "one-inch picture frame." Personal narrative essays and memoirs tend to focus on particular events, people, and critical incidents that frame the writer's life. These do not have to cover the entire trajectory of a writer's life the way that an autobiography does; although they might. Scholarly personal narratives, however, do a lot of the work of autobiographies, personal narrative essays, and memoirs *with one major addition*: namely, SPN writers intentionally organize their essays around themes, issues, constructs, and concepts that carry larger, more universalizable meanings for readers.

Just How Personal Does SPN Writing Have to Be?

SPN writers have the right to choose the level of self-disclosure with which they are most comfortable. I myself have written an SPN that is an extended philosophical argument for a particular kind of teaching.[7] While it is true that I wrote a very personal book, I always kept in mind one rule: how do the self-revelations in my personal story support and illustrate my contention that a constructivist teaching-learning model in schools of education is a valuable one? Thus, I made the decision early on that I would not write an in-depth, chronological autobiography. Rather, I wanted to tell the story of my bumpy, professorial odyssey moving from a philosophy of objectivism to constructivism to an uneasy combination of both during my many years of teaching in the academy. I wanted my more personal self-disclosures to frame the tone and mood of my pedagogical narrative; but I didn't want them to dominate my central ideas. In short, I wanted to write an intellectual autobiography *and* a personal pedagogical reflection.

While writing my book, I was always conscious of using specific, personal events and people in my own my life in order to serve my main philosophical purposes. Some readers liked my attempt to move back and forth from the abstract to the concrete, from the erudite to the simple, in my SPN. Others found my book to be pedantic and hard to read, because of what one of my students called "its big ideas and even bigger words." Ouch! Finding the most salient balance between important intellectual content and honest personal voice is crucial in doing good SPN writing in the academy. Admittedly, the challenge is formidable. But the choice of the proper balance is always up to you, the writer. The reader will let you know whether or not you've been successful.

In contrast, some of my students take more personal risks than I do in their narrative self-disclosures. These run the gamut from being profoundly to moderately personal, from sad to happy, from didactic to understated. Some of these disclosures cover an array of such vulnerable topics as personal depression, harmful religious experiences, child abuse, the tragic loss of intimate relationships, professional scandals, racism and sexism, homophobia, incest, career scandal and failure, and the erosion of hope and meaning. Other narrative self-disclosures emphasize the positive side of writers' lives on all of the aforementioned topics: optimism, spiritual rejuvenation, happy childhoods, the strength of intimate relationships and excellent mentoring, professional integrity and success, social justice, good parents and family life, and the presence of a sustaining meaning found in vocation, relationships, and worship.

In actuality, however, most SPN narratives are a combination of both depth and height, darkness and light. Not all topics are heavy. Not all experiences are dramatic. Not all stories are dire. I believe that there is as much instructive narrative content in the quotidian details of an ordinary life as there is in a life lived always on the adrenalin-charged edge of adventure and catastrophe. Authorial discernment in SPN writing is all about identifying what is serious and what is important in our day-to-day lives, even when our existence seems to be so uneventful as to be dull and trivial; even when what appears to be of no interest whatever to anyone but to our own "superficial" selves.

Another of the important challenges of doing cogent SPN writing is to know where our comfort level lies in describing all of those crises and opportunities that appear with regularity throughout our lives. This comes with practice in developing what for all SPN writers is a very special gift: scrupulous self-monitoring based on an honest self-assessment. To know just how much we can tolerate in telling our secrets and making ourselves vulnerable is the first order of business in doing any kind of SPN writing. I well remember the student who came to me after her dissertation was bound and displayed in a number of venues at my university with this request: "I'm afraid that I might have hurt my mother's feelings. Is there any way that I can change that section where I talk candidly about her worst faults?"

I recall another student, in contrast, a teacher, who wished that she had been more forthcoming in her thesis about her ongoing differences with the leadership style of her school principal, whom she felt was "harming teachers." Although she hadn't wanted to "name names necessarily" in her thesis, she did want to describe in more vivid detail how this principal's approach to leadership managed to completely undermine the morale of her school. He did this mainly by playing favorites among the faculty, and by pitting one group of teachers against another. My student felt that if she had written about this with candor, but also with a proper circumspection, she might have been able to draw larger leadership implications for schools in general.

While I intend to write at length in my last chapter about many of the ethical challenges that often arise for SPN writers and teachers, I will briefly scaffold here some very important *emotional* caveats for educators and students to consider. SPN writing can be emotionally upsetting to many students, particularly to those who might be unearthing buried memories that are extremely painful to recall. Some SPN writers are psychologically stronger than others in the sense that they have already gone through a therapeutic process in order to deal with their problems. Some students may be doing this for the very first time, in print and with a teacher, and possibly with peers. Not all SPN writers choose to explore their dark sides, of course, but some do. We must always exercise exquisite care with those who are opening old wounds in their work.

It is essential for teachers of SPN to be aware of the serious psychological pitfalls implicit in SPN writing. Some writers may need outside professional support, for example, such as David, whom I write about in chapter 4, who wrote about his suicidal ideations; or Pamela, another student I write about in chapter 4, who went public for the first time in writing about her childhood incest ordeal. Occasionally, an SPN teacher will have to make informed referrals to the appropriate clinical professionals if students are experiencing a retraumatization of events and people. At the very least, an SPN teacher must care enough for the personal welfare of each and every writer to check in often with how things are going for the writer. Sometimes all that is needed is a gentle inquiry like: "Would you like to meet with me to talk about anything you are writing? I'd love to process some of this with you, if you need me."

Helpfully, one of the reviewers of this book, before it went to press, recounted for me how she handled these emotional dilemmas with her own students who were doing personal narrative writing, most of them for the very first time. She said: "In my courses, I urge students who write personal narratives, or who share their experiences within a small group, to recognize that they have an ethical and personal responsibility to themselves to pursue or disclose only what they believe they are ready to undertake, and that they consider the privacy and dignity of persons not present whom they include in their narratives." This, in my opinion, is excellent advice for all of us who presume to encourage, and to teach, SPN writing.

But Where's the "Truth" in All of This?: A Quick Primer on Postmodernism

The question above leads me unavoidably to a discourse on postmodernism. But don't worry. I'll promise to be as succinct as I can about a point of view that has produced a never-ending babble of contending voices regarding its meaning, most of which are incomprehensible to the general reader. When the 15th-century Zen master Ikkyu was asked to summarize what he considered to be the highest wisdom, he answered in one word: "Attention." When asked to elaborate, Ikkyu answered: "Attention. Attention."

Although I am not a Zen master, I do know how to give clever, one-word responses to difficult, unanswerable questions. After all, I have been told by some of my students that I am a cryptic professor of the first order. I wince whenever I recall a student summarizing my pedagogy for an audience at a year-end, faculty-student celebration: "Robert's approach to teaching is simply to tell students to take two aphorisms and call him in the morning."

And so, in this cryptic spirit, my own Zen word in response to a question regarding the meaning of postmodernism, with sincere apologies to Ikkyu, is "narrative." I'll even add a few words: Find the person's narrative, and you'll find the person's conception of truth. I'll venture even further: We made up *all* our truths, lock, stock, and barrel. I'll go further still: We believe the truths that we need. Finally, I'll go as far as I dare at this time: Everything that I've so glibly asserted about truth in the previous sentences is itself a created story. How then do you, my reader, know what is true and what is false about what I've said? One more time: The answer is "narrative, narrative." Just find my story, compare it to your own, and decide for yourself. So there.

Now, I'll get a bit more serious. In a series of my characteristic SPN aphorisms, let me summarize my own understandings of the postmodern point of view.[8]

Reality as Stories

We do not live in reality itself. We live in stories about reality. Stories can be true or false based on a variety of criteria: aesthetic, psychological, theological, political, philosophical, scientific, personal experience, and so forth. What makes a story true for all people in all times and places is not simply whether it can stand the test of scientific experiment, or whether it can make valid predictions that can be empirically tested. This story of truth, while helpful to those of a scientific bent, may not be helpful to others of different bents. Truth, in SPN fashion, is what works best for the narrator and the reader in the never-ending quest to find and construct narratives of meaning, both for self and others.

Allow me to tell a personal story here about how composing an alternative story for living my own life actually changed my life. The truth of this story lies in the pudding, and the pudding has been good for me and, I think, for others. For several decades, I struggled with what, at times, was a crushing, incapacitating sense of anxiety and dread. Therapy helped, but not as much as I would have liked. Medications were not yet on the horizon for me. Ten years or so ago, I decided after many months of looking at the story I had actually been living, both inside and outside the university, to try to live a different story. Therapists would say that I was attempting to "reframe" my life's story, and maybe I was. I prefer the term "renarrativizing," and I apologize for its aesthetic ugliness.

And so I gradually began the arduous process of transforming my earlier persona of being the know-it-all, hard-assed scholar in the academy—an overcompensation, I'm sure, for being so insecure—to someone who was more like the Robert I really wanted to become. I worked hard at allowing myself to be more open, self-questioning, more the storyteller and story evoker, more the person who was uncertain of all certainty rather than vice versa; but, most of all, I wanted to be someone who showed that he loved people, warts and all.

This pretty drastic transformation of my life has taken the better part of an entire decade, and it is still in process. Some students who knew me then, and who know me now, say that I have not lost my intellectual edge in the classroom. I have, instead, become "softer and gentler," and my edge has become more "mellow." If this is true, I am not disappointed; in fact, I am happy beyond words. But I couldn't have done this without Richard Kimble.

Who is Richard Kimble? Let me tell you by making a connection with how significant the narrative construction of reality has been in my own life. I have always been fascinated with the original television series *The Fugitive,* a popular weekly melodrama in the early 1960s. To this day, I still whistle and hum the haunting theme song to that series. The gist of this television narrative is simple: a successful, career-driven doctor comes home one evening and finds a one-armed man beating his wife to death. Doctor Kimble is unable to stop the violence, and he is knocked unconscious.

When he comes to, he has been arrested and, on circumstantial evidence, charged with the murder of his wife, a crime he did not commit. He is found guilty, and on the way to prison to serve a life sentence, his train is in an accident. He escapes from the twisted wreck. The detective who is accompanying him to state prison, Lieutenant Girard, holds himself responsible, and he spends the rest of the three-year series trying to track down, and arrest, the fugitive, Richard Kimble.

Obviously this is not high art. It's a formulaic suspense yarn, with a trite theme of popular culture: innocent man runs from the authorities in order to prove his innocence by finding the guilty person. What drew me into this story, though, was how Kimble would move from state to state, town to town, surviving by always looking over his shoulder for Girard, and driven by his unrelenting search for the one-armed man who killed his wife. There was never any rest for Kimble. Each week he would have to reinvent himself in order to keep his real identity a secret. Most of the jobs he held while on the run were low level, in order to survive without calling attention to himself. Most of the people he met were facing crises of their own, and were often too caught up in their own miserable predicaments to care about Kimble's problems. So he became a kind of itinerant helping person, practicing "mind medicine" without a license, so to speak.

What all of these people had in common, however, was that Dr. Kimble had come into their lives at just the right time, always under an alias, and he ended up helping them to resolve their crises in some humane way. Completely enthralled, I watched this series every single Thursday evening without fail. I wondered how this man could assume a new identity so many times; frequently fall in love; become intimately entwined in people's most private lives; help them, both young and old, to heal or to overcome some catastrophe; be loved and accepted by them; and then have to step out of their lives as abruptly as he entered, because Girard was closing in on him.

Did he ever get lonely? What kept him going? How could he walk away on almost a moment's notice from people who loved him and from those he had grown to love? What meta-story did he tell himself while abruptly leaving town on a bus or train in order to follow a new lead on the one-armed man?

It was through psychotherapy much later that I realized Dr. Kimble was my postmodern hero, my fictional doppelgänger. He was making up his life as he went along from day to day. His self-identity was fluid, a congeries of self-composed narratives waiting to be acted out in different locales, depending on the contingencies. Most important to me, however, was that Kimble chose to change his old, hard-edged, career-driven, Type A, physician's approach to life because this was the only way that he could survive three harrowing, unpredictable years on the road.

He met people who would not turn him in because they loved the person he was becoming: compassionate, caring, and more than willing to make human connections, especially during those times when people were experiencing catastrophic turning points in their lives. Kimble had transformed his narrative. Also, even though he was on the run and scared most of the time, he was actually becoming less concerned about who he used to be, more accepting of the person he was becoming and, as a result, more tuned in to people around him.

And if Dr. Kimble could do this, I thought, so could I. After all, in a sense I was on the run from the person I really wanted to be. I was on the run from a blue-collar past. I was on the run from all the fears that I was reluctant to face. In some ways, I still am on the run, but much less so. When the series went off the air in 1966, and the lead actor, David Janssen, died several years later, a piece of me died as well. I am not ashamed to admit this. Although I know it sounds silly, Dr. Richard Kimble, a pop culture antihero based loosely on the Dr. Sam Shepard who was accused of killing his wife in the early 1960s, and on the tragic hero Jean Valjean in Victor Hugo's *Les Misérables*, had become my narrative role model.

Yes, you read this right. If I have successfully revised my anxiety-dread story today, it is due, in no small part, to Richard Kimble, as well as to medication. But Kimble's narrative saved my life, in an era before Prosac, Zoloft, and Celexa. I will never forget him. Now, by whistling, or humming, his television series' theme song almost every day, even on my way to class, I am paying a special tribute to his central place in my life. My whistle is my in memoriam to Richard Kimble. *Requiescat in pace*, Dr. Kimble. My whistle also testifies to the "truth" that the story of *The Fugitive* carried for me, and still does.

The Constructivist Circle

All narratives, and here I am including narratives regarding what characterizes valid research and scholarship in the academy, are as much stories about their adherents as they are by their adherents. Each of us is both constructivist and constructed. The stories we construct then turn around and construct us, and we them . . . forever. I call this the constructivist circle. Locate the personal story of the truth teller, and you will go a long way toward locating what the truth teller really means by "truth."

An undergraduate student came to my office one day to tell me of her "terrific insight" regarding her relationship with her honors thesis advisor. She said something like this: "You know, all this stuff about postmodernism that you've been talking about lately. Well, I tried a little bit of it with my advisor. She and I are so different that I really had no clear idea why she wanted me to write *my* thesis in *her* way.

"I wanted to write a kind of literary reflection by telling a powerful story of loss and survival, with my extended Jewish family as the central protagonists. I wanted this reflection to focus especially on my grandparents who were prisoners at Auschwitz during the Holocaust, and who I consider to be courageous, noble survivors. Moreover, I wanted to write this kind of reflection in order to understand why I identify so readily with being a 'cultural' Jew but balk at being called a 'religious' Jew. In the most important sense, then, I wanted the study of my grandparents to really be a study of me.

"In contrast, my advisor wanted me to conduct formal interviews with my grandparents, leave myself out of the study as much as I could, and then test for validity by doing proof checks of inconsistencies when I analyzed the data coming out of the interviews. I could only react, 'huh'? This all seemed so bloodless and contrived to me. After all, I love my grandparents, and I have listened to their stories for years. I also know what I need from these interviews, and what I would like others to learn from them about their own ethnic heritages. Whether or not my grandparents' stories are inconsistent, or even exaggerated, is irrelevant to me. I only know that they have suffered beyond my worst nightmares.

"For example, I remember my grandfather once saying to me: 'If there is a God, then he is a butcher. He is the Gestapo officer who burned my brothers and sisters. He is the camp commander who spit on my mother's grave. This cowardly God stood idly by, as the smoke from the ovens, baking all those innocent children and adults, curled to his damned heavens. I lost my faith in God once and for all in those death camps, and I found something better: a more enduring faith in the people I love, like you. There is nothing more than this. Everything else is a pathetic fairy tale.' I decided that I wanted to tell stories like this in all their original purity, and then let my readers discover their own truths in them. I wanted to discover my own truth in them.

"Then my advisor, who is also a historically conscious Jew, told me that she was trained as an ethnographer in her graduate studies. She was educated to believe that truth or validity in storytelling is a matter of what can be interviewed and verified through the rigorous cross-checking, and analysis, of data. But then she said something really interesting. She said that if we are to learn the terrible lessons of the Holocaust, then we must learn to separate the myths from the realities, the emotions from the facts. This can only happen, she maintained, if we fastidiously cross-check the interview and historical data for validity so that 'we don't end up with egg on our faces.' In her opinion, scrupulous research was the best way to let readers discover the real truths in these stories of suffering and death.

"It was during that moment when I realized we were really both interested in the same thing. I want to hear stories like the ones my grandparents tell which, I believe, should convey truth on their own terms, whether or not they hyperbolize some of these accounts. This is the way that I was brought up, in a very expressive family, that loves to dramatize. I am also an English major who is drawn to fiction and poetry. To me the emotional meaning of these stories is what's important. To me, the personal meaning of these stories *for my own life* is what's most important. I want to write about this personal meaning.

"My advisor also wants to hear these stories, but she wants to be sure that their account is accurate, so that it won't be dismissed by those people who think the Holocaust is a gigantic hoax, perpetrated by political Zionists in order to create an Israeli state. Once I heard the story of her training and her reasons for doing research, I realized that we were not working at cross-purposes. We were only coming at truth differently, out of the 'gut' of our own personal narratives. We finally reached a narrative compromise of sorts, and I am happy. My advisor became human to me the day that she told me her own 'grammy' lost her life in the death camps. Am I finally getting it?"

I could only answer "Yep, you are. But it all depends on what you and I mean by the 'it' in the question you are asking me. What is your particular 'it' story? I'll tell you mine, if you tell me yours. And please know that I don't mean to sound like Bill Clinton." After my little Clinton aside, I did manage, however, to share with her my own construction of narrative truth that I developed in the first chapter of this book. I talked with her about such postmodern, narrative truth criteria as trustworthiness, honesty, plausibility, situatedness, introspectiveness/self-reflection, and universalizability; along with Jerome Bruner's criteria of coherence, livability, and adequacy.

Narrative Truths

The trouble with trying to discover objective truths in our worlds is that we are constantly distorting them with our narrative truths. The scientist and social scientist who adhere to a truth criterion based exclusively on a value-free weighing, interviewing, measuring, and counting of data are telling only one story of truth. As valuable as it might be, there are several other stories of truth to be told, many as equally valuable. Here is my own truth story in a tiny capsule: no objective, impartial truth ever exists outside of a constructivist narrative. This includes, of course, my opinion about the narrativizing of objective truth. What's the main lesson here: *caveat semper veritates emptor.* Let the buyer of truths beware . . . always.

Does this mean that all truths are equivalent in value? Is postmodernism just another excuse for a wishy-washy relativism? It all depends on your truth criteria. A writer, who is so sure that his lord and savior

Jesus Christ is the "way, the truth, and the life," possesses a truth that he is willing to fight, maybe even die, for. An atheistic scientist I know well at my university is equally sure that unless such a conviction can stand up under the test of rigorous experiment, then it must be discarded or allowed to fall by the wayside. He, also, possesses a truth that he is willing to fight, maybe even die for. Whose truth, therefore, counts as more valid? Which truth should carry the day in academia, or in the lived world outside that all of us, including academicians, inhabit?

Here's my answer, and it's bound to be unsatisfying: It all depends on your story. You see, it's always the story that frames, explains, and justifies your claim to an exclusive truth. There is just no way around this. No matter how convinced, brilliant, or enlightened you are, you can't avoid people asking you the following questions: Says who? Where are you coming from? Why? So what? Why should it matter to me? Sorry, dear readers. The long and the short of it is that I need to know your story, and you mine. Truth starts and ends there, both for you and for me. There is no exit. Sartre was right.

Writing Under the Influence of Our Context Bubbles

Our whys (our truths) to live depend on our hows, whens, and wheres. These, in turn, depend on the ways in which we were raised. Our whys are a product of our peculiar tastes, temperaments, talents, timing, tribes, and training. While we do experience great freedom to make choices in our lives, particularly in the ways that we choose to recompose our stories of meaning, we will always be bounded by the impact on us of our particular genetics, psychologies, histories, sociologies, and tribes of influence. Each of us will live out our stories until our dying days within the universal plot line of contingency, choice, and chance.

Claims to truths of one kind or another are always bound up in our context contingencies. As a teacher, I spend much of my time trying to ferret out the particular context contingencies in my students' writings; and I teach them to do the same. In order to do this effectively, though, I need to know their stories. Good writers, like good ethnographic interviewers, are fine story seekers as well as fine storytellers. Teaching is most vital whenever it, like writing, is narrating. It is not simply telling, training, or shaping; although, at times, it can be all, some, or none, of these.

Framed by this boundedness, our whys provide our reasons to live, to love, to learn and, above all, to accept, even celebrate, our finiteness. Without our personal whys, life, I believe, is severely impoverished. Good SPN writers know that they can most effectively express their truths to readers when they are able to explain the meaning of their whys within the personal bubbles of their context contingencies. SPN writers understand that they can never separate their truth claims from the particular ways in which they have been socialized to recognize truth. Personal context, while certainly not the only factor in constructing truth in SPN writing, is, at the very least, the necessary precondition for understanding the meaning of truth for every single truth proclaimer. And this holds for the scientist, educator, humanist, theologian, philosopher, SPN writer, or whomever. SPN writers know that they are always DUI—driving under the influence—of their context bubbles.

And, so, I often say to students, If you want to locate the important whys in your lives, then write an SPN. SPNs will help you to explore all the relevant contingencies in your contexts of meanings. This is what Socrates' dictum "know thyself" really means. Says who? Says me. And this, for what it's worth, is my truth, framed, in large part, by my own contingencies, with a little verifying research thrown in for good measure. You will learn more about my own contingencies as you work your way through this book. Or you can just decide to skip my personal stuff and go for the scholarship. Your choice will depend on your taste and temperament and, oh, on your story, too. See, I told you.

Contending Truth Narratives

The postmodern perspective understands that all truth perspectives, including its own, are at one and the same time true and false, whole and partial, strong and weak, each in their own ways. We need contending truth narratives and perspectives to bump up against one another, so that our own narratives can be kept honest. I wish that the academy, in spite of its avowals that it does, consistently practiced this perspective. We claim that we are pluralists, and yet we spend entire careers putting down opposing truth perspectives, sometimes snidely, other times self-righteously and, sad to say, cruelly.

On my very liberal campus, for example, I have not heard a single professor openly come out as a George W. Bush supporter, or as a Fundamentalist Christian, or as a libertarian economist. So, too, is it rare in one of my graduate seminars for someone to stake out a public position against affirmative action or against a pro-choice abortion agenda. It's even rarer still for anyone I know on my campus, student or faculty, to come out in active support of the United States's invasion of Iraq. No bumping-up of narratives allowed here—against what we progressives tend to see as reactionary conservative stances, simply beneath the interests of an enlightened, intellectual elite like ourselves.

I've stopped going to most academic conferences in the humanities and in education in the last several years, because speakers are so mean-spirited in their academic presentations. Visit a Modern Language Association conference, or an American Educational Research Association conference some time. I find that there is little or no perspective-bumping going on in these sessions; just endless showing off, self-promotion, advocacy, scolding, jousting, guilt-baiting, and ridiculing. More's the pity, I say. I'll just stay at home and teach my classes, where I can try to make real truth-bumping happen. But whose "real" am I talking about, you might ask? Sit down, and let me tell you my story of "real." Let's do some reality-bumping together. For starters, perhaps we can bump our respective professional-conference narratives up against one another. I'm willing to learn.

No Bottom Lines or Final Answers

There is no SPN truth that goes all the way down to some bottom line, or to some basic foundation, or to some final answer.[9] In matters of narrative truth, there is only interpretation, perspective, point of view, and personal preference. There is no "down" down there, no unimpeachable ground upon which to rest once and for all. Interpretation and perspective are what go all the way down. Truth and reality are infinitely interpretable. So, too, is the notion of "validity." Everything is up for grabs. There is no final word on anything, including, and especially, this assertion of mine. SPN writers may or may not believe in the existence of ultimate, unassailable truths. But they are always on the lookout in their own work to avoid confusing matters of personal temperament and taste with the need to enlighten others about *the truth*—once and for all.

SPN Truth Criteria

Postmodern truth criteria, therefore, include these qualities, among others: open-endedness, plausibility, vulnerability, narrative creativity, interpretive ingenuity, coherence, generalizability, trustworthiness, caution, and personal honesty. That's my take on postmodernism. . . . but only for now. I could easily add a vice versa to each of the above postmodern propositions, depending on my mood and perspective at any given time. Do you remember what Mark Twain said about New England weather? I say the same about postmodernism. If you don't like what I've said about truth and knowledge, just wait a minute. This is the best that I can do on truth. Sorry, or you're welcome, depending on your own truth perspective on all that I've said.

But Where's the Scholarship?

It is important not to be intimidated by the term "scholarship." As an advocate of SPN writing, I want to redefine this word; to stretch it to within an inch of its life, but always with integrity. Etymologically, the word "scholar" goes back to the classical Latin *schola* to the Greek *skhole*. This word originally denoted "leisure" or "play." Thus, a scholar was someone who had the leisure to explore, and play with, ideas; to develop intellectual arguments; to write and teach.

The ancient Greeks used to say that *skhole* was the necessary precondition for wisdom, for knowing how to live. Socrates went one step farther: he believed that one couldn't be a lover unless one had *skhole*. For him, the word "philosopher" literally meant "lover of wisdom." Philosophers like Socrates used their leisure time to create stories in order to help people to become wise—more virtuous, courageous, reasonable, and prudent in their actions. Socrates was a "player" in the etymological sense of the word "scholar." In fact, he did some of his best thinking while kicking back at drinking parties and banquets. Just read the *Symposium*.

So what does this have to do with the role of scholarship in SPN writing? It urges us to think of ourselves as wise and loving people who, like the ancients, have stories to tell that might help others to become wiser. Thus, our personal stories contain within them the germs of many intellectual and experiential truths. At the least, they become the means for conveying our wisdom. At the very most, they can change lives.

"This all sounds well and good," many of my younger colleagues will say, "but can people who write in very personal ways in the professional schools still be considered scholars in the academy? I'm no Socrates, not even close. How will I ever earn tenure, promotion, and reappointment?" My initial knee-jerk response is to retort, "Why not?" Then, I become an irritating name dropper. "Have you ever read personal essays and books written for a larger audience by such scholars as Henry Louis Gates, Jr., Edward W. Said, Robert Coles, Stephen Jay Gould, Lewis Thomas, Carl Sagan, Oliver Sacks, bell hooks, Jane Tompkins (whose SPN book I discuss at the end of the next chapter), Sara Lawrence-Lightfoot, and Mary Catherine Bateson? Are they any less scholars and Pulitzer Prize winners when they are writing personally than when they are writing professionally?

"By the way, let me remind you that all of these scholars eventually went on to win tenure and promotion in their universities. Besides, why do you insist on separating scholarship from personal narrative writing? Isn't it possible that it just might take a scholar to do a good personal narrative, and a narrativist to do good scholarship? At least try to keep an open mind on this question."

My rantings rarely end this type of conversation, however, nor are they meant to. To many of my younger colleagues, I have it made, because I am a tenured full professor who has "paid his dues." Of course I can take more risks than they, they contend. I've already proven myself to be what they think is a "real" scholar. I already have a reputation. I can get away with being "innovative," or "subversive," because there is nothing left for me to prove. I've played the game by the rules, and now I am free to bend the rules. Besides, who can ever take away my tenure or my books, right? they ask. Well, maybe. There are lots of ways for the gatekeepers of scholarly truth in the academy to make a "subversive's" life miserable, tenure, promotion, and awards notwithstanding. But that is another book for another time.

Anyway, the word "scholarship" has always unsettled me; but, admittedly, it has always seduced me as well. When I first heard the term as an undergraduate English major, it was in connection with someone who wrote obscure books and articles in words that were often polysyllabic; in labyrinthine (there's one of those words!) sentences almost impossible to decode; and in a prose style that would invariably induce in me a mind-numbing fatigue. The person who was considered the "scholar" in my major field was the "impartial" textual critic, but never the *author* of the stories that captivated me in the first place. I wanted to know more about the scholar-critic and less about the critique. Occasionally, when a literary critic would drop into his scholarly analysis succulent tidbits about his own personal life, I would immediately sit up and take notice. Now the critic became human. He inhabited a flesh-and-blood narrative of his own.

He became an "author," in what, to me, is the best etymological (L. *augere*) sense of the term: someone who invents or causes something; someone who increases, originates, and promotes. In other words, an author is authentic (a derivative of the word "author"): someone who is an active agent in composing a story; someone who is reliable, believable, and trustworthy; someone who creates and invents rather than someone who sits on the sidelines and only comments on other people's stories; someone who projects a personal, as well as academic, point of view.

In graduate school, many of my nationally renowned professors considered the antithesis of scholarship to be "mere journalism." My professors often spat out this phrase with a dismissive sneer. And yet I still yearned to become a scholar, a real-live expert in a particular branch of study. I wanted, someday, to be a distinguished academic. So, downing oceans of coffee and mountains of candy in order to stay awake at night in my study carrel in the university library, I learned to read (really to skim) the required journals and books in philosophy and educational theory. I also learned to write and speak the technical words that conferred power on people like me. I thought that I was happy and competent. After all, wasn't I becoming more and more like "them"?

I also worked at a big-city newspaper during my undergraduate years, and I got to be very friendly with many of those "mere journalists." In spite of my guilt over possibly being thought of as an intellectual sellout by my professors, I even liked these people. I was especially attracted to feature writers, columnists, editorialists, and sports commentators. Beat reporters didn't seem to me to have much personality. They worked extra hard at keeping themselves out of their reportage, and they were all about garnering the facts. Whenever I broke bread with them, they seemed to be shells without centers. It was only when they got drunk that their cores began to show a little. I liked them much better then.

These others, though, told wonderful personal stories, both in their columns and over lunch in desultory and relaxed conversation. They didn't need a six-pack or a fifth of whiskey to loosen up. They were very much at home in putting themselves in the middle of their storytelling and writing. I will remember, forever, what one of them said to me: "It's the stories that grab their attention, Robert, whether you're a teacher or a journalist. Never forget this. Tell a story and you've got their attention. Tell your own story and you've got them hypnotized. Get them to tell *their* own stories, and you've made friends for life."

This journalist knew the secret of artful communication: it's a willingness to be vulnerable to the other in language that the other understands. Moreover, it's knowing that it's the writer who matters, even more than what is written. It's the teacher at all levels who matters to students, even more than what is taught. It's the students who matter to their teachers, even more than the honors grades they earn. Artful communication brings together writers and readers, teachers and students. It lays the groundwork for us to exchange openly with one another, in Tolstoy's words, "those little daily lacerations and uplifts of the spirit" that fill our lives, and make us all more alike than not.

By the way, the journalist dispenser of this wonderful wisdom was also a full professor in a school of communication in a large, urban university. She was expressing to me in her own language the truth that William Butler Yeats uttered somewhere in one of his poems: "What do we know . . . Only that we face . . . One another in this place." No matter how scholarly or unlettered we are, at some point in time we all feel a need to encounter one another openly about the meaning of all that lac-eration and uplift in our lives. This, dear readers, is the existential condi-tion, and it is universal. Tell me your story, therefore, and I will work hard to find at least an echo of it in my own existential struggles to prevail in my life with dignity, style, and grace.

What is my pivotal point about the meaning of scholarship in SPN? Simply this: *Broaden your construal of scholarship.* Rewrite, if you dare, the currently dominating scholarship narrative in your profession. Use your best creative imagination in doing this. Remind yourself every day that you have the power and the right to compose your own scholarly story. In fact, scholars have been rewriting scholarly stories for decades in a number of disciplines in the academy, particularly in the humanities. In literary theory alone, scholars have radically transformed the methodol-ogy of their discipline. During the last several decades, critical literary theory has moved from the new criticism to the new historicism; from analyzing only the "intrinsic technical qualities" of a work to examining only the "extrinsic" historical and political contexts.[10]

The professional schools, in my opinion, ought to take a closer look at how conceptions of research and scholarship have changed through the years in both the sciences and the social sciences.[11] The rule of thumb has been change or die. Reconfigure your dominant scholarly paradigms and, presto, you reconfigure the very phenomena you are examining. This is also the first commandment of postmodernism: We see what we believe; we observe what we narrate; we transform what we reframe.

Scholarship unchanged easily degenerates into scholasticism. In Me-dieval Europe, religious scholasticism was a narrow-minded insistence on hewing to traditional theological rubrics and doctrines. Scholarship thus became a synonym for pedantry and intellectual domination. The era was rightly called the Dark Ages. In contrast, colleges of education, and other professional schools, could be on the cutting edge of creating an "Age of Light" for professional research and scholarship. One of the best outcomes of ushering in an Age of Light in doing SPN research is that no longer would we feel the need to mimic the scholasticism of many of the social and natural sciences in order to gain legitimacy in the academy. We would be the trend setters, and they would follow; we would build it, and they would come. Imagine.

Here, then, is my own narrative take on the *scholarly* dimension of SPN: You are a scholar if you are willing to play with ideas. You are a scholar if you can build on the ideas of others. You are a scholar to the extent that you can tell a good, instructive story. You are a scholar if you can capture the narrative quality of your human experience in language that inspires others. You are a scholar if you can present your story in such a way that, in some important senses, it rings true to human life. You are a scholar if you can help your readers to reexamine their own truth stories in light of the truths that you are struggling to discern in your own complicated life story.

You are a scholar if you have a passion for language and writing. You are a scholar if you are driven to understand what makes yourself and others tick. You are a scholar if you can feel and think at the same time. You are a scholar if you are willing to allow your students, and your readers, to enter your heart as well as your head. You are a scholar if you can help your readers and students to realize that their lives signify, that they matter more than they will ever know.

Scholarship from a More Personal Angle: To Be a Scholar Is to Be a Lover

After class one week, someone in my writing seminar said the following: "Robert, I still don't get the 'scholarly' in SPN." The question was not meant to be a challenge. Nor was it meant to be a complaint. I am convinced that this person queried me out of a genuine intellectual concern; an itch that needed to be scratched before my student could make further progress in doing the *scholarly* piece of personal narrative writing.

I thought about this question in my car all the way home. I had talked at length about my take on "scholarship" as "play," and I wondered why what I had said didn't register with this student. Likely it was because I didn't say it as clearly as I had wanted to. Perhaps it was because I was still fiddling around with the idea, and needed to think and write about it some more before I nailed it, particularly for myself. Maybe I had committed what I call the "etymological fallacy," assuming that if I can give the root meanings and history of a word, then I have captured its full significance. I do this a lot—maybe too much. It's also possible that my student was still locked into older academic understandings of what appropriate scholarship should be: review, quote, footnote, quantify, qualify; or interview, analyze, conclude, and recommend. All well and good, and certainly nothing for which my student should be ashamed. I had just finished an article on the topic of atheism in the academy where I did all of this myself, except for the measurement piece. And the journal's editor was delighted. As was the readership, according to the number of responses it received.

Suddenly, on Interstate 89, making my way home over the same highway I've driven hundreds of times after classes, a thought struck me. Why in hell do I feel such pressure to redefine the meaning of "scholarship"? Because I was now the official University Scholar, was I feeling insecure about having to be a visible scholarly role model to my colleagues, both junior and senior faculty, as well as to all my students? Was I merely trying to rationalize what comes easiest to me in the work I do here and how I do it? Was I actually feeling a little guilty about not doing what is considered tried and true in the academy? Was I reverting to the older Robert I used to be, and using my newly designated scholarly stature to screw with the heads of university bigshots and snobs, knowing that I actually have very little left to lose if I rub them the wrong way? Probably all of these motivations were at work. I am complicated, and my motivations are always mixed at best.

And then, just before I pulled off Interstate 89 to make my way north on 2A, past the Williston retail stores, past Taft Corner, past my beloved breakfast restaurant, Chef's Corner, to Essex Junction where I live, I remembered an obscure quotation I read somewhere long, long ago. It went like this: "There are only two kinds of scholars—those who love ideas and those who hate them." I thought about this. Yes, the kind of scholar I want to be is someone who is in love with ideas, someone who is in love with those who also love ideas, someone who wants to infect my colleagues and students with a love for ideas. At this time in my life, I believe that I can best do this through teaching and writing about SPN. Some scholars do this in other ways.

My previous incarnation as a scholar was of someone who used ideas to prove his own invincibility and brilliance, and others' stupidity. I reveled, then, in being very good at doing this. It was like taking candy from a baby. I remember sadly, though, the day 30 years ago when my mentor told me she "winced whenever she read [my] stuff" because I "wielded ideas like a rapier" in order to fend people off instead of drawing them close. She was right. It took me a decade and a half to admit to myself that I was a scholar who hated, not a scholar who loved. I wasn't playing with ideas lovingly. I was using them as lethal instruments. I was playing with people's heads and losing their hearts, and mine as well. I won all the major intellectual battles in my seminars but lost all my friends. I also lost my desire to teach and my drive to know. I slept in a lot and thought dark thoughts.

By the time I arrived home from class, I had decided that during the last several years, I have worked very hard to become a scholar who loves. As I pulled onto my street, I did a quick review of some of the most important lovers of ideas who had influenced my own intellectual development: Socrates, who only posed questions to his friends and never wrote a word in his entire life; the Buddha, who sat, thought, loved, and performed good works; Jesus, who told loving stories and never published a sentence; Lao Tzu, who wrote one short book of 81 brief verses that have since changed the world; Confucius and Marcus Aurelius, who wrote about themselves and, in the process, wrote more sagely about the art of leadership than anyone since; Mary Wollstone-craft, who taught me about equality by writing proudly and lovingly about her own life as a female scholar in the 18th century; Nietzsche, my favorite philosopher, who scarcely used a footnote in constructing thousands of aphorisms that have stood the test of time, most of which came out of his own personal lacerations; and closer to the present, Ruth Behar, Anne Lamott, Annie Dillard, and Jane Tompkins, writers I quote frequently in this book, who draw from the pith of their own troubled lives to teach their readers great lessons; and so many others, too numerous to mention, but who come in and out of my life so often that they seem like dear friends, even, at times, like intimates.

So here is where I stand on the subject of "scholarship" right now: it's all about loving ideas so much that we are willing to play with them, to take chances with them, to express our passions about them, to deliver them in some fresh, new ways; to nurture and care for them; and to continually test and challenge them in the company of others. I myself can best show my love for ideas by using stories—about myself, and about others—as a way to deliver these ideas. But, first, I need to show how these ideas really matter to me. Telling stories is my way of express-ing my love for thinking. It's my way, in my sixth decade, to make ideas live, to bear witness to my lifelong love affair with the intellectual life, and to become wiser.

And so, with this fresh insight crystallizing by the second, I bounded up the stairs of my home. I mentioned none of this to my lifelong part-ner, Maddie, that evening, as I wanted to hear about the stories she had constructed to make sense of her own busy day. But I am sure she felt a buoyancy in my mood for the rest of the evening, thanks to my stu-dent's question that had inspired me to reconsider the meaning of "scholarly" from my lover's point of view. Yes, this sounds just about right: I am a lover, and I rejoice in knowing that I am. And I will have it no other way.

A Closing Reflection:
Ruth Behar—My Ideal Scholar

In my estimation, Ruth Behar is a scholar in all the ways that I talk about in the previous section.[12] She is a professor of anthropology at the University of Michigan. She is the author of *Translated Woman: Crossing the Border with Esperanza's Story*, a book, among others, that put her on the personal narrative map in her discipline. She has won a MacArthur Fellows Award and a John Simon Guggenheim fellowship. Behar is a distinguished scholar, and has been for the better part of two decades. But she is still on the defensive among many scholars in her own discipline for encouraging a "vulnerable" observer's approach to doing ethnography. She maintains that unless anthropology is able to "break your heart, then it isn't worth doing anymore." This sentiment, of course, is a scandal to those hardline social scientists in her discipline who believe that empirical investigators must wear bionic masks in order to totally immunize themselves to the distorting effects of human emotion.

Behar is at the stage in her career when she is willing to say to these hardliners: "Says who? And why?" She claims, in contrast, that as an ethnographer, she is always as much the subject as the subjects she is studying. She laughs and she cries with her subjects, especially when they trigger powerful emotional memories in her. Whenever Behar hears her field subjects talk about death, children, poverty, and being wounded, she makes it a point to become an active and empathic participant in the conversation. She herself has experienced all of these situations.

Moreover, whenever Behar hears experts delivering abstract, academic papers at professional conferences, trying to deal "objectively" with powerful life-and-death subject matter, she asks them an embarrassing question: Why is it necessary for scholars to remove themselves emotionally from the real lives of real people? Does this surgical removal of the scholar's self make for a more "rigorous science," or does it herald the death of anthropology as a humanistic field of study? She refuses to don the mask of the dispassionate intellectual when she delivers a professional paper.

At one such conference, Behar talked openly about her personal fear of death, triggered by her shock when she learned that another anthropologist she admired greatly, Michelle Zimbalist Rosaldo, had fallen from a cliff to her death while doing fieldwork. At the same conference, she used this tragic incident to share her feelings about her son, Gabriel, whom she wanted "to throw an invisible net around . . . to protect him from all wounds, all hurts, all fears, all sadnesses." The scholars on her panel, not knowing what to say, could only look at her with puzzlement and, in some cases, with disgust. Some in the audience politely averted their eyes.

Moreover, Behar acknowledges that the fact that she is a Latina Jew, a woman, and a Cuban expatriate obviates any claims she might make to scientific objectivity and omniscience in her fieldwork, especially in those countries that play such an intimate part in her own life story. Her ethnicity, gender, and religion position her, inescapably, at the political center of many of her investigations. Whether she is visiting Cuba or Mexico as a fieldworker or speaking at an academic conference, Behar finds it impossible to "evacuate" her self from her work. For her, there is no dichotomized "self" or "other." There are only "self-self" relationships, both in her private and professional lives. Thus, she deliberately looks for ways to "locate" herself at the living center, rather than at the abstract periphery, of all that she does as an anthropologist and scholar.

So, too, Behar admits that because she is as much a humanist as a social scientist, a poet as much as an ethnographer, and a lover of autobiography as much as of case studies, she constructs her social science scholarship and methodology accordingly. She is both a humanist and a scientist whenever she enters the field or writes an article or book. She refers to herself as a "guerilla interdisciplinarian." On a more personal level, she confesses that she is plagued by serious anxiety—panic attacks that can occur at any time. Also, to this day, she continues to mourn the death of her beloved grandfather whose funeral she missed because she chose to be in Spain doing an ethnographic study. Therefore, she is not ashamed to acknowledge that emotional reasons play heavily on all of her decisions to undertake new anthropological projects.

Finally, Behar understands that because she almost died as a young teenager in a devastating automobile accident that took five lives, but not hers, therefore, all of her work possesses an acute, often pessimistic, existential edge. She is keenly sensitive to her own, and her subjects', human pain and finitude. She knows firsthand how anthropology can "break your heart," because she is willing to allow it to come into her heart. When it does, it unearths her own buried memories of disappointment and suffering. In the end, Behar believes that she is a better anthropologist and scholar because of her vulnerability. In my opinion, her observation is irrefutable.

I want to be the kind of scholar that Ruth Behar is. Even though I am senior to her in age, and with regard to time spent in the academy, she is still my teacher and my model. Even though I have no ethnic consciousness whatsoever because both my parents were orphans who rarely talked about their ethnicity or social class, even though I have never been an expatriated anything, and even though in many ways I am blandly apolitical compared to Behar, I still love her ideas and the way she writes. She skillfully mixes informal prose with scholarly constructions. She is philosophical, political, autobiographical, anthropological, and spiritual all at once. She is able to write for a general audience as well as a specialized one. She writes both from the heart and the head. She is a genuine public intellectual.

Several times in the last few months when reading Behar's book *The Vulnerable Observer: Anthropology That Breaks Your Heart,* I was moved to tears. I felt anger. I experienced an outpouring of empathy and compassion. I sensed that I was in the presence of a personal friend and an intellectual ally, even though I do not know her. I don't even know what she looks like. When, as a "vulnerable" anthropologist, she talked about the "fearsome emptiness of existential freedom," I knew that she was speaking directly to me, a philosophical, kindred spirit.

And when Behar speculated that "only insofar as you are willing to view [your discipline] from the perspective of an anthropologist who has come to know others by knowing herself and who has come to know herself by knowing others," I knew that she was summarizing in a single sentence my entire philosophy of education and life.[13] Here, truly, was my ideal scholar. Here was someone I could urge educators at every level, including all my professorial colleagues, to read at least once a year. Here was someone whose scholarly perspective has the potential of changing the face of academia, especially the face of professional schools like mine.

CHAPTER THREE

Tentative Guidelines for Writing Scholarly Personal Narratives

If you want to write, you can. Fear stops most people from writing, not lack of talent, whatever that is. Who am I? What right have I to speak? Who will listen to me if I do? You're a human being, with a unique story to tell, and you have every right. If you speak with passion, many of us will listen. We need stories to live, all of us. We live by story. Yours enlarges the circle.
    —Richard Rhodes, *How to Write: Advice and Reflections*

I feel as if I am drowning in narrative. . . . What's the point, I want to know. What can we make of this? What difference does it make to education?. . . . Maybe, as I age . . . I am losing existential courage, knowing that I too will disappear into the moments and particulars. I seek the comfort of the large idea, the marker, so long live this, and this gives life to thee.
    —Madeleine R. Grumet, "Autobiography:
    The Mixed Genre of Public and Private"

Writing is easy. All you have to do is sit down and bleed.
    —Red Barber, *Show Me the Way to Go Home*

I need about one hundred fifty drafts of a poem to get it right, and fifty more to make it sound spontaneous.
    —James Dickey, *Self-Interviews*

The Three Most Common Fears of Writing Personal Narratives

Every year without fail, students come to my elective writing course on the first day with three basic concerns. First, they are more than mildly curious about scholarly personal narrative writing. But many are not really sure what the lure is, or whether this is something that they really want to undertake. Some have been told that my course is actually the last resort for those students who are ABD or ABT (all but the dissertation, or all but the thesis). Some have heard their peers extol the genre, even referring to the course as a "life-transforming" experience. These same students have also heard from advisors and friends that perhaps writing a manuscript in a more personal way will motivate them finally to finish their degrees, or complete their undergraduate honors theses, or maybe even get something published. For these students, SPN becomes a kind of miraculous lightning bolt, and they want it to strike them— immediately and painlessly.

Although this advice is well intended, most of my professional students still remain skeptical about the worth of SPN writing in an academic setting. It just sounds too easy to them to do this kind of writing and still be able to call it "serious scholarship." Most don't want to be seen as taking the easy way out. Yet in spite of this fear of being seen as lesser "experts" than their professional peers for choosing to do an SPN writing project, they still manage to show up at the first meeting. Whenever I offer my course, they always manage to come.

Those who show up are what I call the "SPN seekers." Some are eager. Some adopt a cynical, show-me demeanor. Some are cautious. Some are committed. All, however, are hopeful that, somehow, SPN might be the way, the truth, and the life. I tell them immediately that it isn't, it can't be, and it won't be. Most don't know whether to believe me. But I also tell them that if they are willing to suspend their prior beliefs for a semester about what constitutes "serious scholarship," then they might someday be able to do a work that represents the most "serious scholarship" of all.

First, this is a work that actually enlarges the notion of "serious scholarship" to include the most important voice in writing: the author's. In SPN, the writer is as much the message as the message itself. How can the two ever be separated? Who was it who said that it's not only the song that matters, it's the singer. It's not just the words, it's the music. It's not just the writer's text, it's the writer's context, pretext, and subtext. By the way, this last sentence, though not as lyrical as the sentences that precede it, is mine. It's my postmodern way of making music. SPN writing, when it works well, is one way for you to find *your* own special music to do the "serious scholarship" that is so important to all of us in the academy.

Second, many of my SPN seekers don't think they have anything worthwhile to write about. "What's so interesting about my puny little life?" is the message they convey, without exactly using those words. "I've got nothing 'big' to offer. So why should I embarrass myself?" This type of self-abnegation always makes me wince. Why? Because I know that every life is a story, and every story has the potential to teach. As Richard Rhodes says in the epigraph that introduces this chapter: "If you speak [your story] with passion, many of us will listen. . . . Yours enlarges the circle."[1]

In more poetic terms, Henry David Thoreau once said somewhere that the "squeaking of the pump sounds as necessary as the music of the spheres." In other words, your little squeaks have the power to carry equal weight with the cosmos's music. It all depends on your vantage point, your self-confidence, and your power of discernment. Thus, I say let your stories squeak in all their splendor. They will teach, but only if you have the courage to put them into words, to narrate them with pride and enthusiasm.

The denial of the value of the self's stories in an academic setting is born in the command all of us have heard in school at some time: never use the "I" in formal writing. The "I," we have been told, is incapable of discovering and dispensing wisdom without the support of the "them," the certified experts. Messages like these leech the fascinating, storied self out of the budding writer, leaving only the clichéd, and often pinched, stories of experts to recirculate over and over again. My first order of business in teaching about SPN is to do what I think of as "courage encouragement." I tell my students that constructing an SPN takes courage and, in order for them to get there, I have to do a lot of encouraging.

Once you know that your stories count, then you can begin what are the major tasks for SPN writers: identifying and embracing those stories, telling them with gusto, and discerning their meanings for yourselves and others. And be willing to let the chips fall where they may. Phillip Lopate once said something very wise in this regard about writing an essay: "To essay is to attempt, to test, to make a run at something without knowing whether you are going to succeed. . . ."[2] Essaying, you see, is a lot like living a life.

Third, my thoroughly schooled-up graduate students will often say that they have rarely, if ever, written in an SPN genre. Will it be possible, therefore, for them to learn the SPN writer's moves that promise success? Many will comment that they can write a term paper, a research paper, or a literature review "with their eyes closed." They know the templates for these conventional types of manuscripts by heart, because they have done so many of them throughout their long years in formal education. From there, they know from practice that it's mostly just a matter of understanding how to fit some new pieces of the knowledge puzzle into the old research templates; a matter, if you will, of knowing how to pour new research wine into the same old format bottles. (Please excuse my blatant mixing of metaphors.)

Tried and true research formats are good, of course, particularly when scholars are aware of both their strengths and limitations, of what they can and can't do. But SPN is a methodology without a well-established, research template in a professional school. I tell my students that we will pretty much be making up the genre as we go along. In fact, most of what I've learned about SPN writing has come from my work with students. I quote the Talmud: "Much have I learned from my teachers, even more from my colleagues, but from my students, most of all" (Ta'anit 7a).

Although it is true that we can learn a great deal in class from reading published personal essays, autobiographies, memoirs, and other like-minded prose, SPN writing begins with a nagging need on the writer's part to tell some kind of truth. And the best way to tell a truth is to tell a story. A story is always profoundly personal and unique to some degree, never replicated in exactly the same form by anyone else. Your truth may be very different from mine, and vice versa. But if I can hear your truth within the context of your own personal story, I might be better able to find its corollary in my own story.

Anyone who has ever managed a childhood, intimate relationship, education, job, or parenthood can tell a story. Anyone who has ever been a sibling, teacher, friend, or boss can tell a story. Anyone who has ever suffered or rejoiced can tell a story. Anyone who has ever been betrayed by someone, or has been the betrayer, can tell a story. Anyone who has strong (or even weak) political, moral, or religious convictions can tell a story. All of this is simply to say that anyone can tell a story by virtue of having lived a normal life. And, if you can tell a story that is honest, trustworthy, revealing, and close to the pith of your own experience, then you can most certainly write one.

Why is it, for example, that many of us feel so comfortable when telling our little stories in an e-mail? The writing flows easily. We are not even thinking consciously about our style or format. We are simply talking in print, telling tall and small tales, composing our lives in a communication medium that allows us to be ourselves. We narrate in these e-mails in order to record the ups and downs of our existence; in order to scream, or to whisper *I am alive, and I matter, and my stories matter, and you matter, too.* It's easy and it's fun. Our casual musings in e-mails carry the promise of creating an intimate tie that binds author and reader, sender and receiver, if only for the moment. Why can't academic writing do the same thing without compromising its fundamental, intellectual values?

In my opinion, no writing, even e-mail composing, is ever wasted. All of it is practice; the rehearsal for the more formal production of composing acceptable scholarship. What we can put into a relaxed e-mail can also be put into a fresh, academic prose style. I have used several of my old e-mails to jump-start my thinking about a complex issue that I want to explore in more formal manuscripts. I even used one e-mail, sent to me by a colleague, to introduce a chapter that I wrote for my book on the need for administrators and faculty to understand the increasing presence of religious pluralism in the academy.[3] This, in my opinion, was the best chapter in the book, because it was the easiest to write. The e-mail freed me up to shape my ideas in a less stilted, less academic language. Hence, my ideas were clearer and more pungent, or so I've been told.

But, of course, all writing must start with the motivation, and the self-discipline, to actually begin to write. After you finish telling yourself again and again that you are smart and brave enough to write an SPN; and that there is, indeed, material in your life that can edify and/or instruct others, then you need to begin the task by actually sitting in a chair to write. Goethe put it this way: "Whatever you can do. Or dream you can do. Begin it. Boldness has genius, power, and magic in it. Begin it now. Now. Now. Now." Richard Rhodes's take on the same counsel is this: "Whatever your purpose, the best remedy for fear of writing, any kind of writing, is the Knickerbocker Rule: ass to chair." He called it the "Knickerbocker Rule," because Conrad Knickerbocker, a public relations manager, long ago gave him this earthy yet sage advice.[4] He never forgot it.

Ten Tentative Guidelines for Writing SPNs

In this part of the chapter, I will present ten tentative guidelines for writing an SPN. I will be speaking directly to you, my reader. These guidelines are my own. They are still evolving, so think of them as my personal suggestions or proposals. At this particular point in my career, they are the unfinished product of my years of teaching a course on personal narrative writing; my supervision of scores of publications, dissertations, and theses; and countless discussions I have had with authors about scholarly writing. I have also read hundreds of books about writing that have enriched my thinking over the years about how to construct an SPN with integrity and verve. Finally, I myself have begun to write books and articles in this genre.

I call these guidelines "tentative" because I think of them as provisional, as still in the experimental stage. They are nowhere near any degree of finality or definitiveness. I am always learning from colleagues, mentors, students, and critics. Having said this, however, I believe in my heart of hearts that these guidelines, even if followed very loosely, will honor the needs of both the academy and the writer. But, of course, only you, my reader, can make this determination for yourself. You will need to reconfigure these guidelines in order to do full justice to the unique sounds of your own creative voice.

In the two chapters that immediately follow this one, I will show how eight of my students adapted these guidelines in their SPN theses and dissertations. These will exemplify in greater detail what I am trying to say here in more general terms. So, dear readers, be patient—the ultimate SPN payoff is coming, for both of us. Ultimate payoffs notwithstanding, however, the SPN guidelines below are still in flux, and always will be; as will all rules, rubrics, principles, and canons in general. Who says so? Heraclitus and John Dewey, that's who. Who cares? I do. I'm a postmodern philosopher, after all.

Guideline 1: Establish Clear Constructs, Hooks, and Questions

A *construct* is a central theme or message, not necessarily based on empirical evidence, that integrates your material in some orderly way. I often refer to a construct as a "struct." My students think of me as a ruthless construct hunter. I ask, "What's your *con*struct?" so frequently, that I am sure many of them wish that I would just go ahead and self-*de*struct.

Many students have come to me over the years with the following type of complaint: "I can't get started on my SPN. I want to, but I'm like a boat without a rudder. I'm stuck, and going around in circles." What I hear in the subtext is the sound of a would-be writer without an identifiable point to make; not exactly sure of what story to tell, and why, and from what perspective; bereft of any organizing theory or concept—or steering mechanism, if you will.

Here are some construct *questions* to ask yourself, as you begin thinking about writing an SPN: What's important to you in your life at this time? What message do you think that your life sends to others? What pivotal lessons have you learned from living your life in the last few years? What simple advice would you give people who are first starting out in a profession? In a marriage? In parenthood? And so forth.

What gives your life meaning? What gets you up in the morning, day after day, year after year, decade after decade? What convictions do you care about so passionately that you would be willing to go public with them on the front page of your state's daily newspaper? If you were a book, what would be your central theme(s), and what would be its title and subtitle? What special memories about yourself would you want to leave to your loved ones in an oral or written history?

How would you like to be remembered in a eulogy delivered at your funeral? What have you done to change anything in your life, either privately or publicly, small or big? Who do you love, and why? Who do you hate, and why? Who do you fear, and why? Who is your friend, and why? Who is your enemy, and why? These types of simple "evocative questions," asked in order to extract a particular point of view about life from the would-be writer, are potentially infinite in number. What they all have in common, though, is the goal of *focusing* the writer in order to *hook* the reader.

A *hook* is a special device, a lure, that will draw your readers into your narrative and keep them there, whereas a construct is a conceptual guide that keeps your reader focused on the overall point of your narrative. You design a hook, however, to capture your reader's attention. For example, in rock music, a hook is a repetitive instrumental passage, a refrain, that gives it immediate appeal and makes it easy to remember. Elvis Presley's and the Beatles' songs all had memorable "hooks." In an SPN, provocative constructs can hook. So, too, can skillfully told stories. Memorable characters and a narrative arc that keep readers thoroughly absorbed can hook. A critical incident around which to build a story can hook. Authentic dialogue can hook. Sometimes a simple and clear writing style can hook. Other times, it might take a more elegant writing style. It all depends on your SPN's goals.

Anyway, a good, clear statement of what you believe at the outset both focuses and hooks. William Zinsser says that the two most important sentences in any piece of writing are the first and the last.[5] I agree. The first sentence entices the reader to spend some time with you. It also gives you, the writer, at least a tentative direction you can travel. The last sentence means that you have stayed the course and completed the journey. You are there at your endpoint and, with luck, the reader has arrived with you. The last sentence is your final opportunity to convince your reader, and yourself, that the trip has been worthwhile. For an author, the last impression, rather than the first impression, is the most lasting impression left on a reader. But you can't hook unless you focus.

Constructs stake out the territory you will cover in your SPN. Will you be advancing a special agenda? Will you be constructing an extended argument in behalf of a particular perspective, such as an ideology, a philosophy, a way of living, a cause, an ethic, a religion or spirituality? It is important to remember that all points of view start with *questions*. No questions, no positions; no questions, no stories; no questions, no SPN manuscript; no questions, no answers—no matter how tentative.

I recently asked 15 graduate students a single question at the start of a semester-long philosophy of education course: What do you wonder about and why? I found that I didn't really need a syllabus for the course, because this deceptively simple question guided all our work for an entire semester. We returned to it over and over again. "Wonder is good" became our mantra. I strongly recommend a book written in a simple, unpretentious style by a public philosopher who asks similar questions: Christopher Phillips's *Socrates Café: A Fresh Taste of Philosophy*. Go to the café and taste.

Guideline 2: Move from the Particular to the General
and Back Again . . . Often

Have you found the most salient mix of particularity and generality, concreteness and abstractness, practice and theory? Try to avoid emphasizing only *whats* as a way to engage readers. This is the way that too many empirically grounded researchers and scientists tend to write. Concrete examples and details can be fascinating, to be sure. But, in an SPN, every *what* needs a *why*. Every fact needs a hypothesis. Every phenomenon needs a purpose. Most data need insights. Actions need reflection. And they all need an honest personal story or two to deliver them cogently.

But, by the same token, avoid emphasizing only *whys* in your writing. This is the way that too many philosophers and intellectual pundits tend to write. As a result, some of their writings get lost in the academic stratosphere, as do their readers. Generalizations, abstractions, and theories need particulars, concretes, and details to support and exemplify them. Professors of writing often tell their students not to write about humanity, but rather to write about one human being. I would also add this: Write first about your own humanity (or lack of it), and then if you're lucky, you might have something important to say about the humanity of others.

What is the universal appeal in your writing? SPN writing is about thinking globally but writing locally. It's writing that begins from the inside out, rather than from the outside in. Eventually it needs to work its way to the outside, however. If it doesn't, then it becomes merely self-serving: confessional and apologetic, perhaps a bit solipsistic. But when SPN writing is both local and global, it invites the reader to make comparisons and draw contrasts. The key is to practice moving from the provincial to the cosmopolitan, and back again, in your writing. Sometimes these moves can be subtle; sometimes obvious. But, as a writer of SPNs you must always be on the move between two destinations—the particular and the general—if you are to speak with special resonance to your reader.

Notwithstanding the value of moving back and forth between particulars and universals that I've talked about above, readers will still need something with a little more staying power to hold onto after they've read your story. As Madeleine Grumet notes about herself in the epigraph at the beginning of this chapter, no reader wants to disappear into the moments and particulars of their lives. All of us, at some time, seek the comfort of the large idea. We need markers, reference points, and compasses to keep us on track. Thus, SPN writers will need to identify an occasional universalizable marker as they tell their stories.

Guideline 3: Try to Draw Larger Implications from Your Personal Stories

This guideline is closely related to the previous one. Aim for larger life implications whenever appropriate. While you will be telling some pretty revealing and provocative personal stories about your life that will hook the reader, don't just stop there. Use your personal story hooks as a pretext for exploring bigger educational, social, cultural, and political issues. Suggest deeper implications, not just for individuals, but possibly for cultures, groups, corporations, even nations. This might sound grandiose, but, paradoxically, one of the reasons for going *inside* of yourself in an SPN is so that, at least some of the time, you can get your readers to go *outside* of themselves in order to see their external worlds in a different way.

Some SPN writers of a more political bent might take this opportunity to analyze and/or critique what they see as injustices, misconceptions, follies, and self-deceptions in the social world around them. Of course, some readers may not agree with these critiques because they are based primarily on the story of the world that the critics prefer to tell. But in the interests of scholarly integrity, at times you will need to develop the broader, "real-world" (whose "real world?" you ought to be asking) implications of your personal stories. This might entail constructing a social critique whenever it is relevant. It might also entail developing a social action statement, a code of ethics, a political commentary, or an educational policy.

Be aware that your readers are always asking themselves the following kinds of questions: Am I wiser in some ways about my own narrative as a result of reading your narrative? In reading this narrative in all of its glorious (or dreary) particularity, am I able to see any of my own particularity in a glorious (not dreary) way? Is there some greater, or even lesser, social meaning in this SPN that might be relevant for my own situation?

Here is a wonderful proof text, written by Chitra Divakaruni, on the importance of writing stories that touch other people's lives. She is talking about novels, but her observations also hold for SPNs, in my opinion:

> The novel continuously opens into something larger than the specifics that form the boundaries of the story, though paradoxically these specifics must be concrete and convincing if we are to intimate a larger truth through them. Reading it becomes a three-dimensional experience, beginning in the book and ending in ourselves. Such a novel, while it is a mirror of, and a commentary on, a particular event, people, country or time, is on some level about each one of us, our central truth. Each successful novel gives a special flavor and shape—and tone—to this truth, but does not limit it to these.[6]

Guideline 4: Draw from Your Vast Store
of Formal Background Knowledge

Try never to shrink from your own store of formal knowledge, or apologize for presenting the insights of thinkers who are smarter than you, or who make your point better than you do. You may know a lot about several academic disciplines, either through formal training or through personal interest. Don't be afraid of drawing generously from as many of these bodies of knowledge as you can whenever you tell your story.

Also, try to cross several disciplinary boundaries whenever you think these border crossings will enrich or expand your story. What you know intellectually can only make your personal story stronger because your intellect is integral to your personal story. What you don't know can only make your story weaker. Don't be afraid to show off your knowledge a bit, in just the right places; but never try to make your readers feel stupid. There's a happy medium between overwhelming and underwhelming the reader, and it lies in enticing the reader to keep on reading because some of your ideas may be useful.

Try to use your background knowledge to challenge readers to keep up with you, or maybe to pick up some new knowledge along the way. The academic disciplines, when relevant, give personal narrative writers a special credibility in the academy, as well they should. The disciplines have the potential to organize, deepen, and upgrade personal stories. They provide the conceptual cement for creating stories that are intellectually sound, cohesive, and lasting. One question to ask yourself regarding the academic disciplines when you write an SPN is this: Are you disseminating even a little bit of discipline-based knowledge in the story you are telling about yourself and others? If you can answer yes, then you are doing a good thing.

Guideline 5: Always Try to Tell a Good Story

David McCullough, the Pulitzer Award-winning historian, says: "There isn't anything in this world that isn't inherently interesting—if only someone will explain it to you in English, if only someone will frame it in a story."[7] An SPN is most worth reading whenever it engages, or regales, or persuades, or inspires, or teaches, or pleases. Good stories, told in simple English, can achieve all of these goals. At the very least, your writing needs to make a powerful claim on your readers' distracted and busy minds to pay attention for even an hour or two. So tell them a story; better still, tell them several stories. The results are guaranteed.

Your story needs to have a plot, colorful characters, suspense, a climax, a denouement, and some significant lessons to be learned. While writing, you need constantly to remind yourself that as interesting as you think your life is, you have to work very hard to make it interesting to others. The best way to do this is to tell a story with some suspense and conflict in it. Try, whenever possible, to add narrative tension. Keep the reader guessing for a while. You don't need to give everything away in the first few pages or even in the first few chapters.

In all the years that I have been teaching, and reading, students' writings, I am convinced that no hook catches the reader (and student) as powerfully as a story, or better still, a series of stories. This might be because some sociobiologists think the narrative sense is hardwired into our brains. If this is true, then we are hard-wired to make meaning of our lives by imposing stories on our worlds. The etymology of the word "narrative" is revealing. It refers to the ancient Sanskrit *gna* which means "to know"; it also refers to the Latin *narro*, which means "to tell."

Thus, narratives are instruments that help us to know about ourselves and others, and to solve problems; they are also tools for us to tell others about our experiences. The reason why these instruments are part of our brain's structure is probably because they have conferred survival benefits on human beings since the beginning of human time. The use of stories as tools has allowed us to become problem solvers, communicators, and survivors.

Here are a few questions to ask yourself as you construct your SPN story: Is your story a way of conveying some truth that you know is important, something that you have learned about life, love, and vocation—for example, something you would like to share with others? Does your story serve to exemplify and explain your central constructs? Why exactly are you telling your story? Whom are you telling your story to? What will keep your story from becoming just another form of exhibitionism or a passing trifle, entertaining but forgettable?

Guideline 6: Show Some Passion

Stand for something. Even fight for something, but not too aggressively, because, temperamentally, many of your readers will not be aggressive personalities. Try to take a position on something with strong conviction and with palpable affect in your language. Allow your authorial voice to be clear, distinct, and strong. Resist the conventional academic temptation to be "objective"—stoical, qualified, subdued, and distant. It's okay, even desirable, to try to be detached or dispassionate at times; but it's also okay to be fully engaged and excitable. It's even okay to be ironic and wistful.

Life, as every writer knows, is incongruous, complex, and paradoxical. It can bore us, soothe us, upset us, and piss us off, sometimes all at once. Try always, therefore, to be honest. Say what you mean, and believe what you say. But make it a point to leave room for the vice versa that you can always utter after every story that you tell, and every truth that you proclaim, and every sentence that you write. The vice versa will keep you humble. And it will sustain your reader's interest in what you have to say because you won't sound like a know-it-all expert.

Here is one of my favorite writers on writing, with regard to the need for passion in writing—the Pulitzer Prize winner Annie Dillard:

> One of the few things I know about writing is this: spend it all, shoot it, play it, lose it, all, right away, every time. Do not hoard what seems good for a later place; give it, give it all, give it now. . . . The impulse to keep to yourself what you have learned is not only shameful, it is destructive. Anything you do not give freely and abundantly and passionately becomes lost to you. You open your safe and find ashes.[8]

Guideline 7: Tell Your Story in an Open-ended Way

Narrate your story in such a way that it might help your reader to see the world a little differently—not to accept your view of the world, but to accept the fact that others do indeed see the world differently from your reader, and this is good. Don't be too interested in securing any kind of agreement or disagreement on your reader's part. Aim instead for a kind of tentative "maybe you've got something there." An even more desirable response on the part of your reader might be one that says "I'd like to read a little more, think a little more, talk a little more, before I can really understand where you're coming from."

Of course, it would be delightful if somebody were to say that the wisdom in your narrative is so compelling that you have pushed your reader to go way beyond the usual taken-for-granteds. The greatest ego boost, however, would be to hear somebody say something like this: "Your work has been truly transformative! You have changed my life!"

But you can't go wrong if you expect nothing more than the following from your reader: "You caused me to think a little more deeply. I don't necessarily agree with you, but you captured my interest. Even though you and I are poles apart, I think that I understand your take on the world and on your personal issues. Thank you for sharing."

Oh that we might all write in the nonpossessive spirit of the *Tao Te Ching*. Lao Tzu says: "When you wish to seize something, you must momentarily give it up. This is called 'subtle insight.' The soft and the weak in you will always conquer the hard and stubborn in you; and in others as well" (*Tao Te Ching*, Verse 80, Ma-Wang-Tui Manuscripts).

Write softly and subtly. Be willing to surrender your truth to a better truth, if only for the moment, or maybe even for a longer while. Wisdom begins in all that is gentle and generous in you. In order to convince others of your truth, you need first to overcome your writer's hard and stubborn ego to declare your truth as The Truth. When and if you do this, you might even change the world. Or in the ironic words of both Lao Tzu and the Buddha, you only get to keep what you are willing to give away.

Guideline 8: Remember That Writing Is Both a Craft and an Art

Know well what a turnoff a sloppily prepared, carelessly edited manuscript can be, even if the ideas are dazzling. Often, editors of scholarly journals and publishing houses will not even send out slovenly manuscripts for external review. They end up in the circular file, with a terse but polite note sent to the author. More than worrying about getting published, though, do not allow your personal narrative writing to be an excuse for sloppiness. Let your readers know that you take your genre seriously enough to construct your narrative with meticulous care.

Writing is both a craft and an art. The *craft* of writing calls for grit and determination. It is the initial struggle to get something on paper.

It's the down-and-dirty work of trying to translate your half-baked ideas into delectable sentences and paragraphs. It's looking for a way to organize a welter of material into a smoothly flowing, coherent, and engaging narrative. I know few writers who feel that every time they sit to write, it is like taking perfect dictation from God. No revisions are ever necessary for these graced souls. Everything's in God's place, and all's right with the writer's world. For most authors, however, putting that first draft together is a lot more like having root canal surgery without novocaine than hearing God's edit-proof words.

The craft of writing also requires the writer to be disciplined and motivated, and even a little obsessive-compulsive. Serious, systematic writing does not start with the head, hand, or the heart. It starts with the rear end. This part of the anatomy must be placed in front of the computer before the head, hand, and the heart can even get activated. This, of course, is a variation of Richard Rhodes's "Knickerbocker Rule," which I mentioned earlier. I call it my "rear end theory of writing."

Please know that you will have at your disposal an infinite number of avoidance strategies when you first sit down to write an SPN. These include giving in to those sudden yearnings for caffeine and junk food; working out; catching up on the latest stock market report; feeding pets, children, and partners; reading and sending "very important" e-mails; paying a long, overdue bill; checking the status of yesterday's laundry still sitting in the washer; and visiting amazon.com in order to locate the one book that will finally get you started on the SPN manuscript you are so assiduously avoiding.

But sooner or later, if you are serious, you will have completed what Anne Lamott crudely, but accurately, calls your "shitty first draft." Now you can look forward to engaging in the *art* of writing which necessarily complements the craft of writing. This is the continual polishing and tweaking that you must learn to love to give to your manuscripts. Polish and tweak your "shitty first draft" frequently. Rewrite, revise, resist, and recover. Make music out of your noise. Create cosmos out of your chaos. Clean up what one of my students calls that "first-draft, total brain-dump mess." Declare yourself, once and for always, an unashamed, unabashed artist-tweaker. The *craft* of writing can be sheer drudgery. In Red Barber's words, it is sitting down and bleeding. The *art* of writing can be sheer joy. In my words, it is sitting down and preening.

Guideline 9: Use Citations Whenever Appropriate

Lace your SPN with appropriate allusions to cherished texts and quotations. Think of these as your "proof texts," or your signature scholarly references. Learn how to avoid using too many or too few of them. Alluding to too many proof texts means that you actually have very little to say on your own. Alluding to too few means that you have no background for what others have said about what you want to say on your own. The *apt proof text* provides a context, deepens your writing, extends its implications, grounds its insights and, most of all, explicitly acknowledges the contributions of others to your thinking. No author is an island, ever. No author is above needing a little help from others every now and then.

To some extent, writing is about recirculating others' ideas within the framework of the personal narrative that only you are living and narrating. If you are truly honest with yourself, you know that, at most, you will be able to circulate and describe no more than one or two original ideas in all the writing that you will do for all your days. Try to do this with creativity, style, insight, and verve, of course; but also look to the wisdom of others to update and revise your recurring thematic motifs.

The *inapt proof text* cheapens your writing because it is little more than spurious padding, a kind of cheap distraction from the larger argument of your narrative. Avoid the temptation to sprinkle your manuscript with gratuitous quotations from every expert under the sun in order to show off your brilliance. Work instead to achieve the best balance between expressing your own ideas and referring to others for support, clarification, and improvement. Too much academic writing is nothing more than an excuse to drop names, for the sole purpose of showing off one's scholarly pedigree. This is always a bore.

A doctoral student asked me the following question in a somewhat troubled e-mail she sent me late one night: "In a nutshell, Robert, what's the best way to learn how to write? Can anyone really teach me to write an SPN? I'm sitting here staring at writing manuals, and nothing's registering."

I decided, instead of pontificating, that I would share an apt Annie Dillard proof text with her that I have always found eye-opening; particularly when I am blocked in my own writing. It turned out to be a very apt citation, because this student went on to produce an excellent dissertation. Here's the proof text from Annie Dillard's *The Writing Life:*

> Who will teach me to write? a reader wanted to know. The page, the page, that eternal blankness, the blankness of eternity which you cover slowly, after affirming time's scrawl as a right and your daring as necessity; the page, which you cover woodenly, ruining it, but asserting your freedom and power to act, acknowledging that you ruin every-

thing you touch but touching it nevertheless. . . . the page, which you cover slowly with the crabbed thread of your gut. . . . that page will teach you to write. There is another way of saying this. Aim for the chopping block. If you aim for the wood, you will have nothing. Aim past the wood, aim through the wood; aim for the chopping block.[9]

This particular quotation hit the mark with my student because she has always prided herself on being a good, old-fashioned, Vermont wood chopper. She loves engaging in this very physical task, especially when she has a lot on her professional mind. Thus, my choice of a proof text to respond to her question turned out to be right on the money. It might have even cleared the way for a dissertation, because it helped her to "aim for the chopping block" in her writing. No longer did she feel that she needed to hit the bull's-eye in the center of the target each and every time she sat to write. Now she could be satisfied with giving herself over to the page—not to *fight* or to *flee* from the writing but to *flow* gently with it. She was able to write past and through the page. This was, for her, an act of authorial liberation.

Guideline 10: Love and Respect Eloquent (i.e., *Clear*) Language

Your ideas may not always be scientifically defensible, or even erudite. But if you can keep your language somewhat simple—not simple-minded, but fresh, honest, personal, and down-to-earth—then it could get you closer to your goal of being eloquent in your writing. Powerful, fluid, graceful, and persuasive language can cover a lot of mistakes. These four adjectives, by the way, cover the first meaning of the word "eloquent" in *Webster's New World College Dictionary*. I leave it to you to decide how much professional writing you've read in your lifetime that reflects these four adjectives.

Margaret Atwood has said that writers need mainly to answer the following three questions before they start any manuscript: Who are you writing for? Why do you do it? Where does it come from? According to Atwood, attending to these simple questions will keep your language within reach of all your readers, not just a select few. She goes on to say: "Writing has to do with darkness, and a desire or perhaps a compulsion to enter it, and with luck, to illuminate it, and to bring something back out to the light."[10] There is nothing like using simple, clear, direct language as a way to illuminate your own darkness, as well as the darkness of your readers.

In my opinion, Atwood is talking about how to frame an SPN. *Framing* a manuscript is every writer's inescapable prerequisite for achieving even minimal direction, focus, organization, and clarity in a book, dissertation, thesis, or essay. I will add to Atwood's questions my own take on framing, by posing a series of questions that I continually urge my students to think about in writing SPNs. Before they can even begin, they need to be clear about the following: What precisely is it I want to say, anyway? What pivotal questions am I asking? Who is my intended audience? What personal passions for my topic will sustain me over the long run for writing an extended manuscript? Why, in the end, does any of it really matter, either in the short- or long-term?

What type of writing style will I use in order to most powerfully convey the uniqueness of my own voice and views? What in the world might be the personal and/or professional relevance of my stories and ideas for others? Why do I need to say what I do in an SPN style rather than in a more conventional qualitative or quantitative study? Am I looking for an easy way out? Am I at all aware of just how difficult it will be to write personally, cogently, intellectually, and universalizably, all at the same time, in the interests of achieving clarity and eloquence?

In addition to doing some very careful framing (and this could take some time), work frequently on improving the clarity of your writing. Create a signature writing style that virtually shouts to your reader: clarity, clarity, clarity! Strunk and White talk about the importance of clarity in this way:

> Muddiness is not merely a disturber of prose; it is also a destroyer of life, of hope: death on the highway caused by a badly worded road sign, heartbreak among lovers caused by a misplaced phrase in a well-intentioned letter, anguish of a traveler expecting to be met at a railroad station and not being met because of a slipshod telegram. Think of the tragedies that are rooted in ambiguity and be clear.[11]

In the interest of clarity, try to rid yourself of your infernal writing "tics." Everyone has them. Like mine, your sentences might be too long. You might overuse adverbs or adjectives or passive voice. You might be tempted to show off your amazing vocabulary. But style and flash, no matter how brilliant, can frequently get in the way of your substance.

I am not saying that clear writing means you must pretend to have the vocabulary of a 12-year-old. Or that you have to write down to your readers. Writing down to anyone, no matter what the age, always insults them. Neither am I saying that you can never draw on the specialized language of your discipline to buttress your ideas. Too many "experts" on simple, clear writing make it sound as though if you do not write like

Ernest Hemingway or Dr. Seuss, then you are writing incorrectly, or worse, writing like an "elitist."

While I like Ralph Keyes very much, some of his advice on writing simply doesn't hang together.[12] In one paragraph in his book, *The Courage to Write: How Writers Transcend Fear*, he claims that the use of jargon, adjectives, adverbs, passive verbs, qualifying verbs, and run-on sentences are the tools of academic writers who are afraid of coming right out and saying what's on their minds. In the very next paragraph, however, Keyes himself uses 13 adverbs and adjectives, along with at least three passive constructions, and a couple of qualifiers to boot. If all this is good enough for Keyes, why not for his readers?

Keyes does make a very good point, however, when he says that academia rewards those scholars who master what he calls "bafflegab" (passive, vague, abstract jargon) and punishes those who try to write plainly and clearly. He cites many studies showing that academic evaluators rate scholarly articles containing lots of "bafflegab" higher than articles that use more down-to-earth English—even when the evaluators themselves have no idea what the words mean. The more a scholarly piece of writing needs translation, the higher evaluation it automatically receives from scholars. And so the message sent to younger educators in the academy is this: use "dull, difficult prose" in your writing and you will succeed. Use lots of insider words, complex syntax, and endless referencing, and you will be a celebrated, tenured, full professor in no time. Sad to say, in my opinion, Keyes hits the nail on the proverbial head here.

What I don't like about Keyes, though, is that he sets up a false dichotomy: simple = always good; complex = always bad. I disagree. I have found that good writing can be both difficult and clear at the same time, or at different times, even within the same paragraph. Some ideas are just too complicated to grasp in a sentence or two with no word over two syllables; or in a chapter that doesn't require the reader to consult a dictionary at least once or twice. Keyes needs to understand the distinction between technical jargon and an extensive vocabulary. Keyes also needs to learn the meaning of "dumbed down." His own book reflects the rich vocabulary of a college graduate. Reading his fine book, I had to consult the dictionary more than a few times, and I'm glad that I did. He would be upset with himself, but I'm not.

In contrast to Keyes, I contend that good writing means finding the delicate balance that exists between big and small words, informality and formality, long and short sentences, simplicity and complexity, elegance and clarity. A good rule of thumb in writing is this: Does the cogency of your idea drive your use of language, or is it the other way around? If it's the latter, then you've got things backward. Try to achieve a nice complementarity of style and substance in your use of language. This is the work of a lifetime, of course, but it's work well worth doing nevertheless.

Richard Rorty talks about the importance of coming up with live metaphors in your use of language. These, for Rorty, ought to produce "tingles" in the reader. Rorty declares:

> If you want your [dissertations and theses] to be read rather than re-spectfully shrouded in tooled leather, you should try to produce tin-gles rather than truth. What we call common sense is just a collection of dead metaphors. Truths are the skeletons which remain after the capacity to arouse the senses—to cause tingles—has been rubbed off by familiarity and long usage.[13]

Here, then, is a simple rule of thumb for you as you choose the right language to write your SPN: let it produce "tingles" rather than "dead metaphors."

A Closing Reflection:
Jane Tompkins—An SPN Writer Extraordinaire

I first heard of Jane Tompkins when I was studying literary theory many years ago for a graduate degree. She was the author of *Sensational Designs: The Cultural Work of American Fiction*, and *West of Everything: The Inner Life of Westerns*. In 1987, she published a very well-known, and controversial, essay entitled "Me and My Shadow." In this scholarly essay, she intentionally wrote with two voices, her "critic-self" and her "feeling-self." Throughout her text, Tompkins interpolated what she was *feeling* about what she was *writing*. At the time, this was a startlingly new methodological turn for scholarly writing in her profession. This was Tompkins's way of transgressing her discipline's insistence that scholars, particularly women, must write only with their critical, academic voices.

Predictably, some of the criticisms of this piece, by both male and female scholars in her discipline, were harsh. Some, however, saw the essay as a breath of fresh air. Supporters felt that Tompkins had given voice to a new generation of women academics, who refused to accept the academy's rubric that the emotions and the intellect are a lethal mixture whenever one tries to produce "serious" research and scholarship. After all, if Tompkins, who had hitherto built a towering reputation as a "rigorous" literary theorist, was beginning to write more honestly, in direct defiance of the hoary intellect/emotion dichotomy in the academy, then others could as well.

Let me say upfront that I did not especially like Tompkins's two books mentioned above. I found them to be full of the jargon of literary theory and too clever by half. I felt they represented nothing more than the obligatory, academic work of a young professor at Duke University, trying to make tenure in a newly established department of literary theory. There was not a single line in those two books that I wished I had written. This is a rarity for me, because I love the acumen of fine writing, and I often covet an eloquent sentence or an ingenious turn of a phrase.

I was sad while I read these two works, not because Tompkins was playing the tenure and promotion game we all play, but because I sensed she was consciously silencing her powerful, creative voice. I felt that she had something to say but didn't quite know how, or was unwilling to say it. This was the deliberately subdued voice of a writer striving for scholarly authority rather than someone telling her truth and letting the devil be damned. This was also the confused voice of a scholar not quite knowing how to convey her genuine passion about literature, and particularly about pop-culture westerns, to her readers. But when I read "Me and My Shadow," I thought that Tompkins was now on the way to allowing her full human voice to come to the surface in her published scholarship. I knew then that she was starting a scholarly journey from which there would be no turning back.

Much later, though, when I read her 1996 book *A Life in School: What the Teacher Learned*, I knew that Tompkins could never return to a way of writing and teaching that forced her to deny the existence of her "emotions, body, and spirit, as well as mind." I rejoiced. Like some groupie fan, I even sent her an e-mail. Tompkins's *A Life in School* is one of the best SPNs I have ever read. Even though there is not a single footnote in the text (there is a brief "List of Works Cited" in the back), the book pulsates with intellectual energy. Even though the book is not a let-it-all-hang-out, tell-everything autobiography, it is one of the most emotionally honest pedagogical memoirs by a university professor I have seen yet.[14]

I recommend this book highly to those of you who might someday want to write an SPN. It's not the only way to compose an SPN, of course, but it's a wonderful example of a well-known scholar writing within her personal and intellectual comfort zones in order to produce something honest and wise. I admire her courage and her conviction. I also admire her passion, resilience, and faith, the three SPN "writerly" qualities that I will talk about more in the last chapter of this book.

I said in an earlier paragraph that there wasn't a sentence or phrase in Tompkins's two earlier books that I admired. Let me say right now, though, that in my hard-covered copy of *A Life in School* there isn't a single page that isn't dog-eared and underlined excessively. Neither is there a chapter that doesn't feature several sticky notes on the pages. Tompkins's SPN beautifully melds vernacular writing and academic discourse, without a trace of the off-putting technical vocabulary of her discipline.

The story Tompkins told in this 1996 book revolved around her career-long, deep-seated, ambivalent feelings about being situated both inside and outside the academy. Did she or did she not belong? Tompkins wrote extensively about her lifelong battle to confront her fear of authority, and her terror of not being able to measure up to expectations. This terror often left her in a state of "emptiness and loneliness." It also triggered what she called her usual illness repertoire: "butterflies, nausea, hollowness, nagging pain, sharp pain."

No matter how much Tompkins seemed to accomplish, graduating with highest honors from Vassar, and earning a Ph.D. from Yale in American literature, she was rarely able to experience a lasting personal satisfaction. Again, in her words, "At Yale I spent five years learning how to strangle my love, and I never quite got over it." Before she "made it" as a tenured professor at Duke, her life was miserable. She had terminated two marriages. She was "on her third psychiatrist." When she achieved tenure at Duke, she was still unhappy, despite entering into a satisfying marriage to the noted literary theorist Stanley Fish, a union that survives to this day.

It was only when she discovered Fish's postmodern, reader-response theory to reading texts; and feminist activism, that Tompkins felt empowered to start teaching and writing the way that she was honestly feeling. She was in the process of overcoming her long-standing fears. She quoted Krishnamurti in this regard: "Fear is what prevents the flowering of the mind." She also credited T. S. Eliot's *Ash Wednesday* with opening her eyes to the possibility that she could rebound from her "spiritual death" to a "longed-for resurrection." And this she did, completely changing her narrative on teaching. Here was a genuine metanoia. And here was her signature teaching aphorism, in two short sentences: "The longest journey a person can take is the twelve inches from the head to the heart. Who is helping our students to make this journey?"

Here was the story of her transformed pedagogy in a single paragraph:

> I no longer needed or wanted to be validated in a certain way, validated by the authority of knowledge and expertise, by the experience of being the one who talks while others listen. I wanted to be in the moment. And to be there, I couldn't have a program, or a prepared text, a thing that I put in between me and whatever was happening. Between me and the students. The thing—knowledge, whatever—would get in the way.

It was at this point that Tompkins's narrative reached out and grabbed me by the throat and wouldn't let go. Even more, she touched something in me that caused me to rethink my own way of being in the academy. I had already begun to teach the way that I was feeling, thanks to psychotherapy and medication, so much of what Tompkins was saying confirmed my already changed pedagogical heart and mind. But now, thanks to Tompkins, I decided to *write* this way. Why shouldn't my writing follow my teaching? Why shouldn't I be whole? Why was there such a drastic division between my teaching and my scholarship? Was this my problem, or the academy's? Why didn't I just make the decision to write what I felt and believed, and stop second-guessing myself? Why couldn't I write fine sentences such as these:

> As far as the university is concerned, the core of the human being, his or her emotional and spiritual life, is dealt with as a necessary evil, on the sidelines, and the less heard about it the better. We don't want people to think of our students as having problems. But having a problem with your self is the existential dilemma, the human condition. Learning to deal with our own suffering is the beginning of wisdom. I didn't learn this—that is, that I had to start with myself—until I was in my late forties. I could have begun sooner.

Well, I'm here to say that writers like Jane Tompkins helped me to turn the corner on my fear of writing myself as I am now, and not as I used to be, and not as most of the academy wants me to be. Whether this is a departure from a conventional scholarly style that will win me fame and fortune in the eyes of my discipline, colleagues, and students remains to be seen. I've already experienced some fallout, because I refused, after their formal invitation, to serve on the editorial board of the prestigious American Educational Research Association's (AERA) national journal. How dare I, said one of the officers of that organization, turn down such an opportunity! Nobody had ever done that before. Frankly, I find AERA's research norms inflexible and deadly stultifying, and I told them this. To them, there's only one acceptable way to do research in education, and that's to simulate the sciences and social sciences. All the rest is illegitimate.

At this stage of my life and career, put me in the same camp as the irreverent Clint "The Glint" Eastwood when asked how badly he wanted to win an Oscar (he did go on to win one for his direction of the film *The Unforgiven*). He said "I don't give a rat's ass whether I win anything. I just want to be happy, do good work, and be me." Jane Tompkins makes me happy to be me and to do my good work. She does this never more so than when she quotes people who say such wise things as: "You know . . . my whole life I have been complaining that my work was constantly interrupted, until I discovered that my interruptions *were* my work." To which I say, you go, girl, Jane Tompkins! You go!

CHAPTER FOUR

Narratives of Transition and Self-Empowerment

As you go the way of life, you will see a chasm. Jump. It is not as wide as you think.
> —Joseph Campbell, *The Hero with a Thousand Faces*

What lies behind us and what lies before us are tiny matters compared to what lies within us.
> —Ralph Waldo Emerson, "Self-Reliance"

We don't go looking for transition. Transition crashes in on our cozy nests and we are thrown out onto the street to crawl in the gutter, to double over in pain, to carry the full weight of confusion everywhere we go. Transition is an opportunity to take the call. But not everyone does.
> —Nancy Slonim Aronie, *Writing from the Heart: Tapping the Power of Your Inner Voice*

Confronting the Chasm

In this chapter, as well as in chapter 5, I will present eight representative SPNs that students have done for me over the last few years. (These eight have given me permission to use their real first names and to quote from their written thesis and dissertaton work.) I will group them under certain thematic categories. In this chapter, I will talk about four students who have written SPNs with a common theme: transition and self-empowerment. The titles of their works follow their first names in the section headings below. Each of the writers takes a different tack in telling their stories. Ironically, three of them happen to be professionals in my university's athletic department. One is an administrator, one a coach, and one a teacher. The fourth writer is a high-level administrator,

the director of career services, at my university. I chose their work to
analyze, not because of their respective professions, but because their
written works exemplify SPNs of self-discovery and transition. These are
popular themes among certain of my SPN writers, who approach them
from a number of diverse angles and perspectives.

Some of my students confront their chasms by jumping, some by
retreating, and some just by standing there and looking over the edge.
Some spend less time looking behind and before them and a great deal
of time looking at what lies within them. Some, though, look mainly to
the past, or stay with the present, in order to gain self-understanding.
And some experience their more dramatic life transitions as opportunities to take the call.

Others, however, refuse to take the call to change. They prefer, instead, to concentrate on the terrible aftermath of their crises as a way to
tell their stories of failure and redemption. Whatever their differences in
construct, approach, focus, and hook, however, students who write SPNs
of transition and self-empowerment are striving to come to terms with
what Jung calls "archetypal" developmental themes. They are all asking
similar questions about the meaning of their lives: how to negotiate
change and how to become empowered in the midst of it.

KELLY:
"A Personal Account of One Athletic Trainer's Journey
through the Lessons of Life, Learning, and Teaching"

I remember the first time I met Kelly. Tall, poised, smart, and soft-
spoken, she showed up on the first day of my graduate SPN course
looking frightened and confused. She wondered aloud why she was
even there. She said for all to hear: "I'm a certified athletic trainer. All
my courses have been scientific. Not once in my entire undergraduate
career have I written anything using the 'I' word. I know how to do a
scientific experiment. I know how to do a formal research study. But I'm
afraid I will be way out of my element here. Is this where I belong, do
you think?" I let Kelly's question hang in the air for a while.

Thanks to Kelly's outspoken honesty, others also responded during
that first meeting. Some expressed their doubts about taking a personal
narrative writing course because they weren't sure they wanted to go
public with personal content. Some could hardly wait to get started, having already taken a creative writing course or two. The SPN approach
appeared to be an excellent fit. And a few were desperate to find some
inspiration for undertaking a thesis or dissertation to which they could

give their time and energy. These students were experiencing graduate school writer's block because so much was at stake for them. As one said, "It's dissertation or perish for me, and I don't want to die ABD."

As the course progressed, Kelly grew confident. After listening for several weeks to members of the seminar tell revealing stories about their personal and professional lives, she began to take more risks in her own writing. Gradually, her personal story took shape, mostly in fits and starts. But it wasn't until we read Nancy Slonim Aronie that Kelly became emboldened. She decided that she needed to write about what she called her "personal journey into the unknown." The personal story that unfolded from that moment on was nothing short of eye-opening for her and for her seminar cohort.

Here is how she introduced the thesis that she would go on to write:

> This thesis is about what I call my recent "personal journey into the unknown." I find myself frequently reflecting upon the past year and thinking about how much I have changed, and how much I have learned. This particular year was the most challenging, scary, tear-filled, frustrating, eye-opening, and rewarding time of my life thus far. I suppose I had never thought that writing about it might help me gain a new and needed perspective. Much of my undergraduate and even graduate courses have been science-based. I have spent hundreds of hours studying, memorizing, and researching the work and words of others, reviewing textbooks, journals, and attending conferences. Now it is time for me to start using *my* words.

Gradually during the SPN seminar, Kelly revealed pieces of her story to me and to her peers. She was a certified athletic trainer who had left a successful private practice of ten years to go back to school for a graduate degree. She also ended a long-term, intimate personal relationship. She found herself at the university as a graduate fellow with no teaching experience, facing two large classes of undergraduates each semester who were in the Athletic Training Education Program. She was also taking graduate courses in my interdisciplinary program that were unlike any academic work she had ever done.

In brief, her new life was filled with emotional ups and downs, self-doubts and second guesses, and only fleeting glimpses of personal success. As a woman experiencing what adult developmental theorists call the early to mid-thirties transition, perhaps the most tumultuous stage of development for a woman, Kelly felt that she needed time to step back and reflect. She wanted an opportunity to examine the trajectory of her life up to the present. She also needed to establish some goals for both the short and long term. An SPN thesis seemed a perfect opportunity for her to do this, and this is why she decided to continue in my course.

She was encouraged by Nancy Slonin Aronie's words about personal narrative writing:

> Go to the place your mind and your hurting heart are afraid to go. Without thinking, analyzing, philosophizing, every step of the terrified way, without all those trained-to-behave-the-way-they-always-have neurons pumping, without judgments, comes clarification. . . . Writing is your guide to knowing yourself. . . . It comes from your truth.[1]

As Kelly pondered what the shape and content of her thesis might be, she knew that she needed to come to terms with her shyness about public self-exposure. She also wanted to write a thesis with some universalizable and pragmatic applications for others who might be in similar, life-changing situations. She wanted to go to the "place where she was hurting," in Aronie's words, but not in such a way that her writing would look like self-pity or whining. She had too much personal dignity for that. Finally, she wanted her thesis to be scholarly, if not in the scientific sense, at least in the best humanistic tradition.

First, Kelly knew that she needed a centering construct for her thesis. She decided that her life during the last ten years had been about "overcoming a fear of the unknown and the lessons [she] had learned along the way." Thus, her main construct became: "We as educators cannot provide the best environment for learning if we as individuals do not value ourselves and the life experiences that we have to offer. In turn, we must encourage our students to have confidence in themselves and to speak their voice and tell their stories." This central construct helped Kelly to organize the many subthemes in her thesis.

She also included a number of hooks to catch the attention of her readers, such as describing the volatile life of a graduate teaching fellow; confronting "stereotypes regarding turning 30"; and helping women to be successful when they decide to return full-time to college after taking time off for a career and/or family. Her pivotal inquiry questions were: What am I passionate about and why? What story do I want to tell? What will be most challenging and fun for me to write? What is the central thematic motif in my life story up to this point? How can I challenge others to examine their lives in a way that will leave them hopeful and productive?

Second, Kelly needed a way to tell her story that would be both honest and creative, as well as scholarly. After reading Marian Wright Edelman's *Lanterns: A Memoir of Mentors* in the course, Kelly came up with a methodological framework. She decided to write an extended personal letter to "students, educators, and policy makers," not just in athletic training programs but in all professional graduate programs. She also decided that, like Edelman, she would set up her chapters by identifying ten lessons that she had learned along the way.

Her overarching lesson was Lesson One: "Don't let fear rule your life." Other lessons included "trusting yourself to make decisions based on your values, beliefs, and morals"; "It is all right to 'be with the question'"; "Understand that graduate school and teaching can be the most frustrating and rewarding experiences of your life"; "Acknowledge the importance of spirituality in teaching and in living"; and, perhaps the most enlightening lesson of all for her, "In the end, everything always works out." Each of Kelly's chapters provided extensive personal commentary on these lessons.

Third, Kelly needed a way to universalize her insights for other certified athletic trainers. She made the decision to include in her thesis a number of specific policy proposals for undergraduate and graduate athletic training programs both at her university and throughout the country. One of the strengths of her thesis was how seamlessly she was able to combine professional policy proposals and personal narrative. Here's a proposal that was quintessentially Kelly: "Accept that policies and procedures change slowly, but do not give up on making positive changes that will enhance the learning environment. Be particularly proactive, not reactive, when it comes to your learning, teaching, and working conditions." Lots of examples and recommendations followed from this proposal. This proposal, like all the others, was a direct reflection of the personal learning Kelly herself had undergone while going through her graduate program, and starting a new life as a teacher-trainer at the college level.

Kelly also realized that if there was one weakness in her thesis, it was in the area of scholarship. This was ironic for her, because she prided herself on being a rigorous applied scientist, having taken so many science and physiology courses during her undergraduate training. Kelly, like many students who are writing in an SPN style for the first time, experienced difficulty in knowing how to integrate research, scholarship, and relevant proof texts so that these were logically and smoothly embedded in her narrative. She didn't want the scholarly piece of her project to look like superfluous padding, or to break the flow of the story she was telling.

Once Kelly got over her trained compulsion to cite dozens of formal research studies in order to validate her personal insights, she became more comfortable with the scholarly dimension of SPN writing. She learned how to refer to her own professional and personal experiences in order to validate her observations. She was still learning how to use supplementary quotations from appropriate readings and studies to deepen and enrich her insights. In SPN writing, a proof text reference serves only to enhance and add something to the writer's text. It never becomes the central pivot of the text, unless it acts like an epigraph. Epigraphs function mainly to dramatize, preview, and/or highlight the personal tone and message of the text. Kelly understood that with more practice, she could become a fine SPN writer, someone who would be a personal narrativist, scholar, practitioner, and teacher all rolled into one.

During her formal thesis defense, Kelly presented her proposals to more than 50 onlookers, including students, faculty, and the university's athletic director. What they saw and heard was a peer professional unafraid of talking about her personal life in public, and also willing to draw larger professional implications from her own experiences. Her audience listened attentively as she presented ideas for a transformed curriculum and pedagogy in athletic training education. This would be a curriculum, by the way, that would encourage students at both the undergraduate and graduate levels to write scholarly personal narratives as a part of their professional training, in addition to more conventional scientific writing.

Kelly received a rousing ovation when she finished. Many of her colleagues and students in the audience were thrilled that a fellow professional in their midst, someone with whom they interacted every single day, could actually write a graduate thesis that exposed so much of herself. Even more, they appreciated that a faculty committee at their university would give such a thesis enthusiastic and unanimous approval. Even the athletic director declared publicly: "Maybe we should require all our students to write scholarly personal narratives." I noticed that Kelly's face immediately brightened when she heard this. She had won the public support of the university's athletic director. I knew that she would be the first person to volunteer her services as an SPN teacher if she were asked.

Finally, Kelly wanted to conclude her thesis in such a way as to bring her narrative full circle without having it lose any of its story line or its tension. She decided to use an extended roller-coaster metaphor. Here, in her own words, are the climax and denouement to her story of self-empowerment and her overcoming of fear:

Just this past summer I went to Universal Studios in Florida and found my favorite roller-coaster yet—the brand-new, massive, purple-and-green, Incredible Hulk thrill ride. As the car started the slow climb up the long mountain of steel that was encased in a metal tube of darkness and neon lights, I turned to my left to tell Tim how much fun this was going to be. Halfway up the track the car catapulted up the remainder of the tunnel and shot us out into the daylight only to be instantly inverted before plunging downward towards the hundreds of tourists mingling in the park below. The best part about this ride was that it completely surprised me. It was new and different and scary and exhilarating, and I loved it. I have since accepted that my life (just as learning and teaching) today is much like that of a roller-coaster, and that looking forward to its surprises, twists and turns, is something to be excited about rather than fearful of. Ultimately, through my course of graduate study, I have learned there are many things that I cannot control, and although at times I may want to slow the ride down, I do not want to get off. I am trying something new. My eyes are wide open, and although I am kicking and screaming along the way, I am enjoying the ride. And I am still learning.

DAVID:
"Embracing Human Suffering—
Toward an Emotional Pedagogy"

David had taken several graduate-level courses with me before he enrolled for my SPN seminar. Slight of build, long dark hair pulled back in a ponytail, intense, often inscrutable, and complex, David at times baffled me. I yearned to know his story. What leaked out in his previous papers and comments only whetted my appetite to know more. He would sit and stare at me, and at others, for long periods of time in my classes, always with a poker face. He never seemed to blink his eyes. I was unable to read his nonverbals. It was clear that I was auditory, and he was visual.

I knew that he was from Oklahoma, that he had been a child development major as an undergraduate, that he was a tennis coach at the college level, and that he had a mixed ethnic background, including a Native American heritage. I also knew that he was a baker, an animal rights activist, an excellent tennis player, and a devout vegan. David presented himself as a person who lived simply, close to the rural land, and as someone who loved to learn. I liked him almost immediately, although I could never tell what he was thinking. For a long while, I could not sense if the courses he had taken with me were worth his time and effort. I wondered, because I could always count on David to express his unorthodox political opinions in classes, without pulling any punches. Why, then, wasn't he being as forthright with me?

David and I became friends during the time he was experiencing a series of crushing personal crises. I remember listening to him talk openly after one of my summer courses about many of the psychological issues he was facing, and desperately trying to overcome, during that period in his life. I was pleased that he had sought me out to discuss his personal struggles. I felt accepted and trusted. I listened, and I marveled at his inner strength and gentle nature.

As a personal aside, I find that I'm drawn to students who trust and like me, regardless of how well they do in my courses, or what they believe, or how they look. I once said to a group of students who seemed particularly distant from me one year: If you like me, I'll like you back. If you don't, I'll go out of my way to treat you fairly, but I won't choose to hang out with you. Predictably, this pathetic little self-revelation of mine fell on deaf ears. The distance between me and them grew even greater. One of my more candid colleagues, upon hearing me complain about the poor state of my relationship with these students, said this to me: "Duh! What do you expect, if you are in the habit of saying such dumb things to them. You sound too needy. I wouldn't want to hang out with you, either." She was right, of course.

Anyway, David and I eventually got close, probably because I never said anything so dumb to him. At least, I hope not. David was a superb writer. As a word stylist, he was a natural. He had a great feel for honest and simple language. He was a fine metaphorist. He wrote from the heart as well as from the head. His personal candor was unflinching and courageous. He could tell many wonderful and moving stories about himself. I recall thinking after reading one of his papers that a writer like David comes along once or twice in a professor's lifetime. He was so gifted that he made me feel like a writer whose main talent was merely to cut and paste well. David didn't cut and paste. He created, composed, and risked . . . greatly.

When it came time for him to think about a thesis topic, David decided that he wanted to write about existentialism and the emotions. We had talked about this philosophy in depth in one of my courses, and he was hooked from the beginning. He realized that he had always been an existentialist, and now he had a name to attach to his developing philosophy of life. Now he also had a framework for looking at his past, and how he might want to live his life in the present and future. He no longer felt lost intellectually. The task that lay ahead for David, though, was to find a sharp thematic focus for his thesis. He also needed to craft his personal narrative in such a way that it would speak to educational practitioners, including coaches. Finally, he wanted to write his thesis about existentialism as an applied existentialist. What research style, therefore, would be most suitable for this project? he wondered. He soon found that SPN fit him like a glove.

Here is how he described the SPN approach in his thesis:

> I write in the first person. The concept of the personal narrative has been explained to me the following way: Our own experiences are equally as valuable in terms of research as quantitative or qualitative measures might be. Each one of us are rich encyclopedias, full of history and future, draped in a moment called the present.

In my opinion, a more concise definition of SPN has yet to be written. In fact, I wish that I had said this.

David chose as the primary construct for his thesis the need to embrace human suffering with courage and faith, an existential theme common among such philosophers as Søren Kierkegaard and Paul Tillich. David spent much of the first part of his thesis telling the story of his own personal suffering. He did this because, in his words, "in order for me to truly connect with the pain of the Jew and the slave, it is imperative I search for the root of the suffering in my own story. Empathy in itself will not suffice. Instead, we who bleed must bleed honestly, willing to do so in front of the whole world."

In the bulk of his thesis, David talked about his early childhood abandonment; the breakup of his parents' marriage; the terrible, lasting trauma of having been repeatedly raped by his stepfather; his frequent psychedelic drug use as a young man, the breakups of his marriages, and the "near miss" of committing suicide, among other serious life crises. His narrative was a gut-wrenching chronicle of a life full of tension, suspense, real characters, misery, and struggle. The strength of David's SPN writing was his ability to narrate a master story, as well as a number of subsidiary stories, that literally reached out and "touched my heart," as one of his committee members remarked to me.

Not once did David write about any of the above-mentioned life events in such a way as to elicit sympathy or pity from the reader.

Rather, he had more important goals in mind, because his SPN was actually meant to be a study in personal growth, redemption, and transformation. There was always the promise of hope and resolution in David's SPN, even during his account of the worst of times in his life. He wrote his thesis as an evolving existentialist who had slowly come to the conclusion that he must become an active agent in composing his own life; in transforming the meaning of his suffering. David recounted how, with the help of a skilled psychotherapist and a great deal of support from his university community, he went on to build a life as a very successful tennis coach, as a graduate student now enrolled in a doctoral program, and as an existential educator-coach.

Throughout David's thesis, there were several wonderful existential insights. Here is but one example:

> I have grown weary of living in a community where I stumble when others glide, where I listen intensely and yet words have little meaning. I want to replace visions of suicide with walks through the park, where my lips kiss innocence, my eyes see children in glee, my skin feels the beauty of the spring breeze. I want to be seen by the bus driver from a mile away and coach my tennis team with the vigor they deserve. I want to embrace my alienated state not as a curse but instead as the fundamental trait of my authentic self. . . . I believe all of this to be possible. I believe the answers lie in a very intriguing place, one that Sartre refers to as the "magical world of emotion."

David chose as his central existential construct for the applied piece of his SPN this proof text from Robert Solomon's book, *The Passions:* "We are responsible for everything we do, and everything we are. And this includes our emotions."[2] Having accepted the truth of Solomon's quotation for his own personal struggle to be authentic, David attempted to fashion a pedagogy of emotions in his thesis. By citing a number of authors on emotion, including Daniel Goleman, Van Cleve Morris, Hazel Barnes, George Kneller, and others, David took the first step to create what he called an "emotional pedagogy."

Today, David acknowledges openly that the *professional* universalizability of his SPN was not as strong as his personal and philosophical narratives. At the time of the writing, he hadn't been able to achieve enough distance from his own story in order to construct a practical, teacher-useful pedagogy of the emotions. This will take time and further reflection, but I am convinced that it will eventually happen for David.

Generalizability in an SPN is one of the most difficult moves for a writer to make, particularly for a writer-scholar like David, whose journey of self-discovery and reconciliation has been so profoundly painful. It means consciously going outside the self, beyond the enormous stresses and turbulence of an intimate personal story, in order to create transfers of meaning for others. Perhaps when David gets more perspective on his own story, he will be able to frame corollaries of professional meaning for others, including educators and human service professionals.

Here is how David ended his thesis:

> I wear my truth like a scarlet letter. Possibly, I am exaggerating my newfound freedom of expression, but I don't think so. What I have attempted to do in the pages of this text is to live by what I believe in. I no longer have anything to hide; nothing that awaits me can be kept from my eyes or tongue. I mean the things I have said and will continue to find greater meaning in each of them. . . . In conclusion, I announce that the world lies ahead of me, awaiting my choices of the day. Like a possibility hand-drawn by Sartre himself, I know it is I, not they, who are at the helm of my destiny. A professor once asked me "when will you leave the hill [in the out-of-the-way rural area] where you live and will yourself to power?" I now respond in honesty: I like it up here. I have a wonderful view of the world. Things are just fine.

JOE:
"A Lost Season—
The Nature, Culture, and Prevention of Athletic Team Hazing"

Joe was once a student in my interdisciplinary master's program. For several years, however, I lost track of him. He had chosen to withdraw unofficially from his graduate program due to his increasing responsibilities as first assistant hockey coach for our division one university hockey team. The work pressures on Joe were growing more intense to recruit, travel, manage, and coach. Joe was overextended. He decided to put his graduate education on hold until his life settled down. In all honesty, though, I never expected to see him again. But then, with a single devastating incident, Joe's life fell apart. As a result, he returned to graduate school, and to my program, to lick his wounds, to reflect, and to build a new life for himself. The thesis he wrote became a personal narrative of abrupt transition due to a life-transforming crisis, and the gradual, near-total reconstruction of a professional self.

It is important to set the stage here. Joe had been an extremely proud Vermont undergraduate ten years earlier, with a major in English. He was also a varsity hockey player as an undergraduate. His ties to the university were strong, as a student, alumnus, and former elite athlete. A Minnesotan, Joe came to the university on a hockey scholarship, a real coup. Hockey at my university is the crème de la crème of competitive sports, and scholarships are highly competitive. There is no football team at this state university, and so hockey "rules," as Vermont high school students like to say.

Moreover, hockey throughout Vermont is the unofficial state sport, overshadowing even football and basketball. Just about every high school in the state has a varsity hockey team. Hockey is everything to young athletes in Vermont. No other sport even comes close. When the call came for Joe to become an assistant coach at Vermont, he and his family made the decision to return to his alma mater and to settle in the Burlington area. Life was good; the possibilities were unlimited. And then any coach's worst nightmare happened!

An extremely serious hazing incident took place with the hockey team during Joe's time as a coach. This was an incident that produced a media frenzy of epic proportions throughout the state of Vermont. When the dust had settled, in Joe's words the tragic aftermath included "graphically detailed allegations of hazing in the state's major newspaper [almost every day], two lawsuits, investigations by the university and the state of Vermont's Attorney General, the cancellation of the final fifteen games of our season, hostility all around, and many deep psychic wounds." This incident, according to many insiders, was also the cause of the eventual resignation of the university's president, Judith Ramaley.

Regarding the personal impact of this terrible hazing event on himself, Joe wrote:

> For these reasons—my years of personal involvement, my struggles to help make the team successful, and my pride in the program—what happened last year was deeply painful and profoundly humbling. I felt under attack and became very defensive, and it was some time before I could step back and take a more objective look at what had happened.

Joe's SPN thesis was his opportunity to sift through his own feelings about what occurred on that fateful day, as well as on all the days that followed. Many in my state considered this to be the worst scandal in the university's athletic history. In his thesis, in addition to recounting all the grisly details of the actual hazing event along with its public aftermath, Joe also looked critically at many of the larger, social and psychological aspects of college hazing. A considerable portion of his work in the thesis included detailed analyses of the available research on athletic team hazing. Finally, Joe made a series of recommendations aimed at preventing future hazing incidents at his alma mater.

The challenge for Joe in writing his SPN was to blend together his personal story, his insider's candid analysis of a highly publicized scandal that reached several national publications, his critical review of the pertinent research literature on hazing, and his drawing up of a series of recommendations that he hoped might forestall future athletic hazing episodes at the university. Among the macro questions he asked were, What is hazing? Why does it persist, particularly in collegiate sports? What are its upsides and downsides? Can hazing be prevented? What role can education play in changing the cultural norms that reinforce hazing behavior? Joe's explicitly stated central construct and conclusion were:

> While it is too early to say anything definitive about lasting effects on our program, I honestly believe the ordeal our team has been through will make us stronger as a group and could ultimately be a positive step for our program. This has been an opportunity for us all, players and coaches alike, to step back and reevaluate what we do and how we do it. In the process of this reexamination, we have learned something about commitment to our goals and to each other, about discipline on a large and small scale, about how to treat people with respect, and about what is really important in life and what is mere distraction . . . We may have unwittingly allowed our players to grow too comfortable with their status as a high-profile team in this community. Being knocked around like we have over the past several months has humbled us all and has helped us to tighten our focus on what each of us needs to do to be successful.

For me, the most powerful message in Joe's thesis was the one that rarely surfaced explicitly in his text—the one that existed mainly in the subtext, implied but not explicated. This was the submerged message that, in my opinion, was the most crucial: *How did Joe himself feel about all of this?* Where did he find the courage to pick up the shattered fragments of his life and go on? What philosophical, interpersonal, and spiri-

tual resources did he draw upon during the time he was forced to confront what existentialists call a major "limit situation"? Limit situations
push us to the precipice. They test our moral mettle. They force us to
make choices about how to deal with issues of life and death, suffering
and loss. How did Joe manage to face and heal what Tolstoy called the
existential "lacerations" that occur in every person's life at one time
or another? Are there implications in Joe's situation for those of us
who must deal at times with our own professional and personal limit
situations?

Joe's special achievement as an SPN writer, in my opinion, was to
construct an almost nonpartisan iteration of most of the key events in
the hazing scandal. He also was able to convey in an incisive prose style
the catastrophic effects that the hazing incident had on so many people's
lives, including his own. In a sense, Joe told a riveting, insider's story of
an event that, at the time, affected many people throughout the state
of Vermont, and still has major reverberations several years later.

Joe did his best to respond to some of the more personal existential
questions that I raise in a previous paragraph. He mentioned his disappointment over the abrupt termination of the season. He expressed his
personal concern for the psychological state of his beloved head coach
who knew nothing of the hazing incident. He talked of his disenchant-
ment with his team when they "misled" investigators early on. He mentioned his fear of losing his job. He was honest in admitting that he
bore "some resentment" toward the chief complainant on the team who
brought the lawsuit against the university. He mentioned his concern
about having his "honesty and integrity publicly questioned," and he
admitted that "I have even questioned my own sense of purpose and
worth as a coach and educator." He also confessed that he "began to
seriously question my commitment to the 'ideal' of competition."

Moreover, Joe pulled few punches in his thesis. When he felt that
members of the team had lied to interrogators during the posthazing
investigations, he said so. When he felt that the coaching staff, including
himself, could have handled things differently, he said so. When he felt
that the university administration had erred in judgment, he said so.
When he needed to express his own personal anger and frustration at
the situation, he did. Joe's integrity and candor came through on every
single page of his thesis. He wrote what he is: a young man of incredible
moral character, a throwback to the days when elite athletes did not consider themselves to be anointed as God's chosen people, with a free pass
to do as they pleased with no accountability to anyone but themselves.

It's important for me to say at this juncture, however, that just because I wanted to read more of Joe's personal story in his thesis, he did not have a writer's obligation to tell such a story. The degree of personal self-disclosure and self-probing in SPN writing is always the author's choice, not the reader's. Joe narrated exactly the story he needed to, for a variety of reasons, at the time he wrote it. This is good enough for me and, in my opinion, it should be good enough for his readers as well.

One lasting impression I have of Joe is the courage and dignity he displayed while defending his thesis before a large audience in a meeting room in the athletic complex. This group included his former hockey mentor and head coach; the assistant athletic director; a number of prominent university coaches, faculty, and administrators; and many friends. Treating every single person in that room with exquisite respect and care, and without faltering, Joe narrated his story of the hazing scandal as he himself had experienced it during the darkest days. He also took a strong position on what he thought needed to be done in the future so that hazing incidents would not happen again.

Joe's message was hard to hear, I'm sure, for many in that room. I know that it was difficult for some of his fellow coaches to hear, because a few told me later. But he spoke his truth with humility and compassion. And he left all of us with something very special: one highly credible, insider's interpretation of the meaning of a cataclysmic hazing event that had occurred during the month of October 1999 at the University of Vermont.

Where is Joe today, and what is he doing? Here are his own words toward the end of his thesis:

> The turmoil has taken its toll. To be successful [as a coach] and to thrive in this environment requires a tremendous investment of time and energy, a fervent love for the game, a very strong will, thick skin, and above all, a commitment to competing intensely on a daily basis. For me, this is an investment and a commitment that I am no longer willing or able to make. At this stage in my life—with a wife who works full time and two young children—the job of Division I hockey coach is no longer compatible with my life goals. Not long ago, I figured out that I spend in excess of two months out of each year away from home recruiting, playing games, or otherwise traveling for my job. . . . By the time my children reach age twelve, I will have missed a full two years of their lives. . . . I do not wish there to be such a cost to my family for the sake of winning hockey games.

Joe eventually resigned from his coach's position, resumed and finished his master's degree studies, wrote his thesis, and is currently enrolled in a doctoral program in educational leadership and policy studies at the university. He continues to live in Burlington, Vermont, and is the life skills coordinator for all of the university's student athletes. In this position, Joe acts as an academic advisor; educational programmer; and general resource, counselor, and support person. He has also become a nationally recognized authority on hazing in college athletics.

PAMELA:
"Living a Life Beyond Fear—
A Narrative Exploration of College Career Counseling
and Student Affairs Professional Preparation"

Pamela came into my life almost 20 years ago as a graduate student in our Higher Education and Student Affairs Administration program (HESA). She was of mixed Colombian heritage and self-identified as a Latina woman. Pamela was bright, a former English major, an excellent questioner and, in my classes, very animated and very enthusiastic about engaging in critical discourse. Although I don't remember this, she tells me that one of my written comments on a paper of hers was so critical that she went through the HESA graduate program convinced that she would never be a scholar. Of course, I believe her account because I tended to be insensitive in those years. But it still makes me sad to think that such a vibrant, intelligent human being would take my callous comments and construe her graduate school narrative in the way that she did. Perhaps this explains why she became a bit more guarded in my courses as time went on.

I got to know Pamela a little better over the next several years during her tenure as the director of career services at my university. Although we were never close, we were always amiable. It was when Pamela entered our doctoral program in the late 1990s that I got a chance to know her much better. And when she approached me to advise her dissertation, I was thrilled. Here is how she described the current state of our relationship in the acknowledgments section of her completed dissertation: "In the nearly twenty years I have known [Robert], he has been a demanding professor, an ardent supporter, a trusted colleague, and a gentle friend. He has provoked from me some of my best writing and clearest thinking." I mention this acknowledgment up front not to convince my readers that I am a good dissertation advisor, but because I am pleased that I no longer scare the hell out of students like Pamela.

Also, I deeply appreciate the last three phrases she used to describe the current state of our relationship: "demanding," no; "ardent," "trusted," and "gentle," yes, particularly "gentle."

Here is how Pamela described her first encounter with me about the direction her dissertation might take:

> During the course of our conversation, I told [Robert] I had realized years ago that fear was a pervasive emotion in my life. I was and am afraid of most things, but I have spent a lifetime exercising the muscles that allow me to proceed in spite of my fear. . . . As I talked to this man who had over the years alternately evoked feelings of fear, respect, and awe from me, and who had inspired, provoked, and encouraged me, he did what he often does. He asked me a question that broadened the conversation beyond the fear. Was my dissertation a journey from fear to something? What did I think was the *opposite* of fear? . . . I would continue to ponder this question for the next couple of months. During that time, I read Jane Tompkins's memoir on teaching, *A Life in School: What the Teacher Learned.* She wrote "my fear has been replaced in a general way by faith, faith that things will work out and that if I pay attention to the moment . . . I'll be all right."[3] That was it! For me, the opposite of fear is faith. My dissertation is about many things, among them my personal journey weaving between fear and faith. . . . This recognition that fear can be transformed by faith, even into love—love of self, of others, of life—provides me with fuel that fires my professional practice.

Much of Pamela's dissertation was about confronting, and working through, some of the fears that have haunted her for most of her life. As she says, "one of the stories I will tell in this paper is about fear, transformed by faith into loving action." Her dissertation was a rich tapestry of personal vignette, courageous self-disclosure, reflective interlude, and a critical examination, and reframing, of much of the current research on career counseling. What made the whole work cohere, however, was the self-empowering way in which Pamela had confronted a series of transitions in her own life. Hers was a story that reminded me of the title of one of Paul Tillich's finest works: *The Courage to Be.*

In my opinion, some of Tillich's comments on courage characterized the philosophical gist of Pamela's work very well: "Courage is the knowledge of what is to be dreaded and what dared." "The courage to be is the courage to affirm oneself in the face of fate, suffering, and death." "Courage is facing one's own finitude, particularly as it gets expressed in anxiety and fear." "Courage is the continuous attempt to avoid despair by making a leap of faith that there is meaning amidst the meaninglessness."[4] I ask you to remember these quotations as you read about Pamela's struggle to achieve self-empowerment in spite of all that has happened to her.

Pamela, from the very beginning of her dissertation, led from her strength as a writer and speaker; she was the supreme storyteller. In fact, whenever I think of the letter *N* in SPN, I think instantly of Pamela. I can't think of anyone I have ever had in my courses who captivated me with her stories as much as Pamela. Storytelling is a special gift, even though, as Pamela pointed out in her dissertation, it is a natural means of communicating for all human beings. We all tell stories, it is true, but only some people are able to mesmerize and inspire. Pamela was one of those people.

In addition to mastering some literary tools like metaphor, analogy, description, internal dialogue, and imagery in her dissertation, Pamela also knew how to do something that is of the utmost importance in shaping an effective SPN. She was able to construct a compelling *narrative arc* in all of her macro and micro stories. This was an arc that had a clear beginning, middle, and end. Her narrative rose and fell in just the right places. It also included the appropriate amounts of character development, suspense, climax, resolution, and denouement.

The end of Pamela's stories was always in doubt, and this was good, because it was difficult to predict their outcomes. Pamela kept her readers guessing and surprised. She also knew how to generalize larger meaning from all the stories she told, no matter how prosaic or extraordinary they might have sounded on a first reading of them. Pamela chose all of her stories very carefully in order to advance each one of her constructs. She was especially adept at using her stories to hook her readers. Whether she was talking about her family upbringing, her performance at school, her adolescent boyfriends, the death of a dear college friend, a career counseling session with a student client, or the meaning of adult vocation versus career, she had a way of seizing, and holding, her dissertation committee's attention. She was able to do this, I believe, because she never delivered her accounts in flat, academic jargon. Because her personal experiences were so trenchant, so, too, was her use of passionate, everyday language to describe them.

Every single person on her committee told me that they found Pamela's narratives to be the heart and soul of her dissertation. One committee member, a bit of a skeptic about the academic worth of SPNs, told me later that Pamela had impressed her "beyond words." She said:

I will never again be able to read a more conventional dissertation in the same way without asking the writer to tell me
some personal stories so I might better gauge where the re-
searcher-self is situated. And I'm going to insist that, in the
future, all qualitative researchers include at least a small personal narrative section where they can come clean with their
biases and baggage.

Pamela's stories were real, and while each one of them could stand on
its own, each also stood for something else—some explicit or implicit
meaning that connected with all of us and helped us to understand her
constructs better.

I will mention just one of these meta-stories, because, in my opinion,
it represented the source of all the fear that Pamela had experienced in
her life up to then. It is hard for me to know just how much to narrate
here, as I want, most of all, to protect Pamela's privacy. But all that
follows is what Pamela included in her own dissertation, which is now
a public document. I will try to be discreet. Remember, however, that
while this self-revealing account was undoubtedly important in the
larger scheme of Pamela's life and work, she also had many other stories
to tell in her dissertation. Among them were stories about the meaning
of "work" and "vocation" in a postmodern age, and the importance of
using narratives as instructional tools in student affairs professional
training programs, as well as in doing career counseling. These latter
two stories, in fact, constituted the core construct in her dissertation: the
best way to serve clients is to get them to share their stories.

In terms of Pamela's background, she was born in South Carolina's
low country, near Charleston. Because of her Latina heritage, occasionally someone would refer to her family as "mud people." Her father was
a sailor on a nuclear power submarine, so he and the family moved a
lot—14 moves in ten years. Her father was the unquestioned authority
figure in her paternalistic home, and everyone did his bidding. Whatever
he said was law. He belittled all of his daughters whenever they talked
about attending college. In fact, he felt that none of his daughters be-
longed in college. And he didn't mind telling them so publicly on many
occasions.

Thus, Pamela lived out most of her subsequent education in a narrative of unconsciously trying to prove that she was worthy of getting
a college education. At some level, she continually sought her father's
approval. She graduated from high school near the very top of her class,
was voted student of the year, and named the most outstanding student.
She went on to win many college scholarships. At the University of

South Carolina, she elected a double major in English and psychology. Her achievements in college were as dazzling as those in high school had been: Phi Beta Kappa, a dozen honor awards, and she was named the outstanding female graduate. However, Pamela accomplished all of this without dealing openly with the one personal trauma that ruled her life—the "success" story she was writing about herself was really a story calculated to avoid coming to grips with the single major, unresolved issue in her life.

This meta-story began with a substory. Pamela wrote about her seventh-grade science teacher whom she liked very much. One day in class the students dissected a frog. Pamela described the scene in these words:

> The frog writhed, soft, white belly up, pulling its pierced feet from the cardboard again and again. As one of the boys made the first cut into the frog's belly, and I saw the beast's body jerk and struggle, I cried out loud and begged her to remember to pith [anesthetize] it. . . . Sharply, she told me to shush my silly girl shrilling and watch the heart beat. I felt scared, hurt and misunderstood, but in that teacher's look, I had learned she didn't know what pithing was.

This simple story was rich with "layers of meaning" for Pamela. But the most important meaning occurred to her 30 years later, while working on her dissertation. Listen to Pamela:

> Years ago I had cried for that writhing, tortured frog. I cried out loud as the helpless creature lay exposed and suffering. My heart went out to the beast, and I was told to hush. Why did it mean so much to me? I have squashed bugs without a thought; even set fire to anthills. . . . Of all of the memories I had of school and teachers, why did I need to keep writing this one? What more did the story have to tell me? . . . Thirty years [ago] there was something else going on in my life. It was something unspeakable, and I had never connected the frog to my history. . . . At that time, I was regularly being sexually molested.

Pamela went on to tell the story of how her father had begun to touch her physically when she was 11 years old. She described how her father was "grooming" her step by step over a two-year period for eventual penetration. Each time he became bolder. "The touching escalated to unambiguous sexual assault" when she was 13 years old. Pamela's description of the assault was frightening in its detail. Not thinking of herself, she immediately wondered if her father had assaulted her siblings as well. After this terrible sexual attack, Pamela heard her father saying to her: "Don't tell your mother. Don't tell your mother about this, okay?" Eventually, Pamela did tell her mother. This put a strain on the marriage (which eventually ended), but it stopped the sexual abuse. Nevertheless, the trauma it caused in Pamela went unresolved for 30 years, even though she had "come out" as an abuse victim to a number of friends and therapists. Her dissertation was the capstone of her cycle of recovery, because it helped her to uncover, and acknowledge publicly and permanently, the impact that her father's violence had on her for three decades of her life.

Pamela spent only ten or so pages in a 180-page dissertation talking about this incident. I focused on it here, not just because I considered it the most dramatic self-disclosure in her dissertation, but because I believed it set the stage for so much of what she had to say about her own narrative approach to life in general and to career services in particular. Recounting the story of her sexual abuse in her dissertation was Pamela's way of demonstrating in her own life the meaning of her central construct: "Bringing our narratives to consciousness and analyzing them teaches us to become better observers of ourselves, and more active participants in the authoring of our lives."

On one level, Pamela's willingness to confront openly and candidly what for Catholic Latino families like hers was the unmentionable domestic sin was an act of purgation and agency. It enabled her to name the horror of incest that had always been a zealously guarded secret in her life, and then let it go. It also forced her to reauthor her life; to compose a very different type of narrative where, in her words, she was no longer a *"victim* of incest. I was on my way to becoming a *'survivor,'* and eventually a *'thriver.'"*

Pamela told a number of additional traumatic stories in her dissertation, including the death of her dear friend while in college. Blair was a gymnast and All-American diver, who suffered a debilitating, and ultimately fatal, accident on a trampoline. During the terrible six days that followed his accident, Blair never lost hope or became "self-absorbed or bitter." It was this tragedy in particular that taught Pamela the "story of courage, of character, of transformation." Pamela recalled the words of Viktor Frankl: "Suffering is an ineradicable part of life. . . . the way in which a man [or woman] accepts his fate and all the suffering it entails, the way in which he takes up his cross, gives him ample opportunity— even in the most difficult circumstances—to add a deeper meaning to his life."[5]

The point of such stories as these was not for Pamela to present herself as the hapless pawn of fate, as just another casualty of life left wounded and dying. Rather, for Pamela, stories like these helped her to live her life more as an active agent:

> Stories help me grow. As I understand my stories and yours, and the stories I read in newspapers and scholarly journals, I understand you and myself better. I become more aware, and more able to assume responsibility for writing today's story and reframing yesterday's, all in the effort to move to being better able to love and live in community with others.

When it came time for Pamela to defend her dissertation, over 70 people filled a room to overflowing to hear her. She stood in front of an audience that included friends, family, coworkers, administrators, and faculty, and calmly narrated her meta-stories. Pamela talked perceptively about her in-depth research on developmental theory and the use of narrative methodolgy in career counseling; and she explained her reconfigured application of this methodology in her own work. But more than that, she did something, which in my mind, was equally as important. What had the greatest impact on her audience was the way in which she told her personal stories of weathering the storms of transition in her life, and learning the lesson of self-empowerment. And this lesson, according to Pamela, had incredible transfer value for all the clients she had ever worked with in her career counseling. She could much better empathize with the storms of transition in college students' lives. She could also encourage them to persevere and to use those crises to recompose their narratives of life and vocation.

Every person in her audience, including myself, was transfixed by Pamela's presentation for the better part of an hour and a half. I swear that I could hear the sounds of people's breathing, so still was that room. I know that, at times, I could hear my own heart beating. Pamela was no longer afraid. She had found the faith and courage to write her narrative, and to tell it, not defiantly, but gently. She had transformed her fear into love and compassion.

Conclusion:
Transition and Self-Empowerment

Kelly, David, Joe, and Pamela, like most of my students who write SPNS with themes of transition and self-empowerment, are trying to find just the right words to describe who they are struggling to become as they recompose their life narratives. They are also exploring how they might best be able to weather the gathering storms of having to face, and eventually overcome, the Sturm und Drang of major life transitions. Each of the four is living in a unique narrative with a different set of characters, plots, challenges, climaxes, and resolutions.

Kelly needs to find the best way to deal with her "personal journey into the unknown." She has fashioned a story of herself as someone who decided to leave behind the comfortable certainties of her past life in order to plunge ahead into an unknown and frightening future. Her special task of self-empowerment in her SPN is to discern the reasons why it was necessary to turn her earlier, comfortable life upside down in pursuit of new experiences, new truths, and new adventures. As I read Kelly's thesis, I was constantly reminded of Blaise Pascal's insight that the heart has its reasons, which reason does not know. Kelly, once the professionally stable, career athletic trainer, but now, at age 30, a student and fledgling teacher of undergraduates, is finally learning how to listen to the world with her heart. I believe that her work as a professional educator can only be enriched by her new-found heart knowledge, particularly those in- and out-of-class relationships she will continue to have with students and colleagues.

David's journey to self-empowerment is equally challenging. The narrative David is constructing for himself is one of leaving his existential angst behind him by reclaiming his authentic self and abandoning his victimized self. His task is to learn how to embrace his human suffering and alienation in such a way that he can recompose the story of his life into a narrative of self-transformation and courage. He needs to make his rightful claim on the world. This will take a major act of metanoia (a radical change of heart and mind), and David knows this. It will be the continuing work of a lifetime.

One of David's section epigraphs, quoted from the work of Hazel Barnes, is revealing: "Bad faith is a lie based on cowardice and fear of the human condition." David's refashioned story of the self includes the insight that he will no longer choose to be a coward. He alone is responsible for his life: for what he does, who he is, and what he feels. In my opinion, David is well on his way. He is currently in a doctoral program in educational leadership and policy studies; involved in a stable, loving relationship; and teaching and coaching as a respected, existential mentor to all of his students and athletes.

Joe, the disillusioned hockey coach, suffered through an extremely painful transition at the university, a transition that could easily have destroyed him, as it did some others I know. I can't help but believe, however, that Joe's strong sense of his multiple and shifting self-identities saved his life. Joe's narrative included a self-understanding that he was more than just an athlete and a coach; he was also a parent, a husband, an educational leader, and a teacher. Thus, his "lost season" never threatened to become his "lost life." In fact, one could say that Joe found his life by giving up his life; or, better, by enlarging the narrative possibilites in his life.

Finally, Pamela, the career counselor and college administrator, needs to continue taking Paul Tillich's words to heart. Courage and faith are inseparable. The courage to be is rooted in the faith that, in spite of all the suffering, life has meaning. Moreover, self-constructed stories confer agency, and love is all. Courage is self-affirmation and a negation of fear. Like faith, courage is a leap into the unknown with no guarantees. It is a leap to connection—with intimates, colleagues, and students—requiring, above all, a willingness to become vulnerable to the other. Pamela, of course, understands all of this. The key will be for her, and for all of us, to remember it when once again our courage is tested by fear. I, for one, am confident that Pamela will remain courageous and faithful, because, in one sense, her whole life has been a rehearsal for her next test.

CHAPTER FIVE

Narratives of Authenticity and Connection

Now I become myself. It's taken time, many years and places. I have been dissolved and shaken. I have worn other people's faces.
—May Sarton, *Coming into Eighty: New Poems*

The ultimate conflict in education is who we are when we encounter and are swallowed up by the artifical world of academia, our fleshly selves slumbering in hard chairs, and how does this strange ritual come to mean anything to us. Our private lives occur in terrifying places where we grapple alone with the impossibility of certitude or peace. Teaching those conflicts means addressing that, opening the windows of academia and letting life seep in like air.
—Abby Bardi, cited in Susan Handelman, "Knowledge Has a Face: The Jewish, the Personal, and the Pedagogical"

When I invoke the personal as pedagogy, stance, or style, what I am really endorsing is connection, between student and subject, teacher and student, reader and writer, student and student, coursework and the work of the discipline and the world.
—Diane P. Freedman, "The Scope of Personal Writing in Postsecondary English Pedagogy"

We Profess Who We Are by the Way We Live Our Lives

Many students who sign up for my SPN course have one objective in common. They are most interested in constructing stories that might heal the rifts that exist between their personal and professional lives. They want congruence. They seek wholeness. They are tired of compartmentalization. What they do as professionals is inseparable from who they are, and who they are striving to become. Whenever I read their narratives, I always find a common, central theme, and it can best be summed up in the following words: "Now I wish to become whole."

Moreover, educators who write SPNs tend to think of their work as a vocation, as a calling. They think of themselves as being called to service; as doing something far more fundamental than transmitting technical skills to their students, or simply managing schools and school districts, as necessary as these basic competencies might be.[1] As professionals, they know that, before all else, they are called upon to "profess" a belief or faith in the power of connections and relationships before all else.

This includes fostering relationships between "student and subject, teacher and student, reader and writer, student and student, coursework and the work of the discipline and the world." Susan Handelman says it well as follows: "For in the end, what are we all about but to facilitate each other's illuminations, to recognize and confirm each other's faces?"[2]

The four narratives that follow, two by teachers and two by educational administrators, reflect Abby Bardi's insight: "Our private lives occur in terrifying places where we grapple alone with the impossiblity of certitude or peace." What Bardi is getting at is a truth that the SPN writers in this chapter are on the way to discovering in their ongoing narratives. Making connections in education is many things, of course, but above all it is about "opening the windows of academia and letting life seep in like air."[3]

Furthermore, the SPN writers in this chapter understand that for them to be the best educators they can be, they must first realize that education is a valuable end in itself, not a mere means to other ends. Schools and universities are places to practice the virtues that everyone agrees are life-giving and life-sustaining. They are places where human beings learn how to be authentic as well as competent, whole as well as specialized. They are places where educators and students put becoming and being on a par with knowing and mastering. They are places where people stand *for* something without standing *over* others. They are places for connections that are mutually vulnerable and mutually respectful. Most of all, though, they are places where professionals profess who they are and what they believe mainly through their actions, less through their declarations. And because of this, students learn who they want to become.

DAVE:
"Who Am I and What Am I Doing Here?—
Postmodern Education that Supports Identity in a 'Normal' World"

Dave showed up in my SPN course during the very first semester of his graduate studies. He was a teacher and educational coordinator at a private, secondary school in the largest county in Vermont, Chittenden County. Dave began his studies in another graduate program, but decided along the way to transfer into my interdisciplinary program. The leading qualities of temperament I would use to describe Dave are intensity, passion, candor, critical intelligence, and just a touch of revolutionary fervor. Lean, slightly balding, and hyperserious in demeanor, Dave presented a persona wiser and older than his 29 years. If I were a believer in Buddhist rebirth, I would call Dave an "old soul."

Moreover, in the first few weeks that I knew him, Dave had a way of making everything he said in class sound like a proclamation of pedagogical certainty. Whenever he spoke, I visualized exclamation points, rather than ellipses, at the end of his sentences. During the semester, he worked hard to correct what he felt was a misimpression of his self-presentation in a seminar. In actuality, Dave wanted to open the conversation rather than to close it. He wasn't sure how to do this, however. He succeeded by the course's end in learning how to speak in the language of "conversation starters," not "conversation stoppers." Many of my graduate students never quite master this conversational style, or this writing style, but Dave did, to his great credit.

At times, though, his palpable passion for learning could be daunting, both to me and to others. I saw him as an insatiable human sponge sitting in my seminar every week waiting for precious drops of wisdom to absorb and make his own. Why not? he would ask. After all, he was in graduate school to learn. It was his quarter, his telephone call, so to speak. He wasn't there to waste time. I couldn't help but agree with him. I grew to like and respect him immensely, as he went on to take several courses with me. Most important, he became my friend: less the protégé and more my colleague in the educational venture.

Dave's special challenge in my seminar was to learn to relax a bit and be a little more patient. It didn't take him long to learn how to return the question to questioners. He did this in an open-ended way, rather than rushing in with fervent answers based on a progressive ideology of education. He learned how to be a participant observer in seminar conversation, often more the observer than the participant. When Dave caught on, it didn't take long for him to feel that he had found the right educational mileau for his unique style of learning, teaching, and writing.

If anything, Dave tended to thank me and his peers too much for everything that he was getting from us. I think it took him a while to fully appreciate that he was actually giving us as much as he was taking. Over time, I admired the fact that Dave's generosity toward others far exceeded his ego needs. In fact, I envied this in him, for I doubt many people would pay me the same tribute. Someday maybe, but not now.

Dave's master's thesis was an extended personal reflection on his "search for meaning" as a teacher. In his own words:

> This thesis is my story. Or as Mark Edmondson wrote in his book, *Teacher*, "This is a memoir; as such, it is my truth, the way it is for me."[4] It is a depiction of my own, individual search for meaning. As evidenced by the citations, many in the field of education have intersected my Truth with theirs, both in theory and practice. However, these separate Truths, I'm sure, run apart more often than they run together. My manuscript is written in the form of a scholarly personal narrative. . . . I believe this form to be the only possible genre in which to convey my ideas, while, at the same time, maintaining a tight grip on my general philosophies regarding education and life.

One of Dave's central objectives in his thesis was to reexamine the notion of "truth" in education from a postmodern perspective. He had once been given a pin by a workshop facilitator featuring the words "Teach the Children the TRUTH." The word "TRUTH" was capitalized and in bright red letters. After the usual, brief period of post–workshop euphoria, Dave began to think more deeply about what appeared to him, in retrospect, to be indefensible claims to the possession of a "final truth." He was becoming a postmodern interrogator. Why was it, he wondered, that so many educators, at so many levels, claimed to be in possession of indisputable pedagogical truths? How could they be so sure? He wished that he could be as certain about even one small truth about teaching as they seemed to be about everything.

Much of Dave's thesis was his attempt to put these upper-case Truths, whether educational, philosophical, political, or religious, under a postmodern microscope. Along the way, Dave adeptly described the ups and downs of his own search for a truth that he could believe in and live. Although the general content of his thesis might sound somewhat abstract, Dave's postmodern inquiry was always grounded in his own concrete teaching and living experiences. Here was Dave's guiding construct:

> For me, the meaning of human life boils down to this: a search for self. The purpose of life is to live in accordance with what we find, and what we feel, during this search. . . . The postmodern search for self never fully stops. Thus, our purpose is never stale. It ebbs with our darkness and flows with our light. Teaching, for me, is to live in accordance with my search for self. It brings me inner peace. I believe it is what I am supposed to be doing. . . . I believe that the life of a student, a learner, must also be cased as a search for self. *Together,* [for both teacher and student] *the end of education becomes this search for self* [italics his]—this individual journey, taken together—to find what matters to the person, as well as to the community.

Dave spent the better part of his thesis tracing his own search for an authentic self from college onward. For most of his college experience, he lived a life of distracted hedonism. Gradually, he began a period of intense introspection, asking all the usual existential questions about the meaning of life, particularly society's expectations for "normal" behavior. After an aborted attempt to pursue alternative teacher licensure in Vermont, Dave began seriously questioning the meaning of "normal" pedagogy, according to the teaching profession's standards. Dave's lengthy account of his failed experience with a standards-driven, teach-by-the-numbers, bureaucratic licensure board was both humorous and sad. He was humiliated and insulted during the board's grilling. Here are his words describing his letdown:

> On the surface, my ALP (Alternative Licensure Program) process was a disappointment. It made me feel like I wasn't a teacher; like I was a big phony. The "panel of my peers" lambasted me into forgetting any professional confidence I had acquired from the people in my everyday life. . . . The letdown was, initially, a knockdown. But to wallow in that misery for too long would be to contradict everything I have been talking about. The ALP process positively defined me, and . . . motivated me to become the professional I am today. It motivated me to make my school the best institution of its kind. And it motivated me to focus my professional efforts on being myself, rather on becoming "normal."

Dave used the experience of his licensure failure to issue his declaration of pedagogical independence. He decided to become a teacher on his own postmodern terms. He chose to teach English in an alternative, private school in northern Vermont where students got placed "due to their inability to comply with public school rules and norms." Here, teaching competence was measured by a very different set of criteria, based on a commitment to the qualities of authenticity, connection, innovation, experimentation, diversity, the quest for personal meaning, and group treatment. In many important respects, Dave and his colleagues transformed the original school. In large part, though, they found themselves making it up as they went along.

There was very little precedent for creating such a school in the state of Vermont where there are relatively few alternative secondary schools. Dave, and other teachers, ended up constructing an educational narrative that was radical in its vision. Theirs was the story of a school where *all* the constituents were expected to be kind, respectful, and committed to the peaceful resolution of conflict—all without compromising either high academic standards or high expectations of acceptable social behavior. Here was how Dave reflected on the rebuilding adventure in his thesis:

> That entire experience was, and continues to be, incredibly liberating. And, as I came to find, definitively postmodern. Our own day-to-day perspective became our Truth, and the Truth of our school. We were shaping personal and institutional identity, and being positively recognized for both. Incredible. I helped build a school—helped give it spirit, helped give it breath, helped make it unique. I helped give our school an identity.

The largest section of Dave's thesis was his explication and analysis of this school's humanistic-progressive criteria for pedagogical excellence. The most fascinating piece of this account for me and his thesis committee, however, was to read how Dave evolved personally and professionally into a 21st-century postmodern educator; and, from his perspective, how others might do so as well. Dave had made a self-conscious decision to become a postmodern educator. From then on, he resolved that his teaching would go hand in hand with his philosophy of life and education. There would be no more teaching versus living dichotomy in his life. He would teach who he was.

What does it mean to be a postmodern educator? I beamed with pride, of course, when Dave quoted me in his thesis. Unashamedly, I include this proof text here:

> Each student's search for a usable and sustainable set of truths is always and everywhere an unpredictable, difficult, and challenging process. All students need our wise and sympathetic assistance, not our omniscient interference, in this demanding endeavor. Just the way we do, they, too, need to form their own sets of values in order to inform their own lives in their own best ways. In the most important sense, of course, this is the point of any and all education, and, truth to tell, in most respects, we [teachers] are merely beside the point.[5]

Dave's postmodern perspective was based on his assumption that "no person has cornered the market on Truth. . . . Yet, to fulfill my vocational responsibilities, I need to explore with my students *some* version of *some* truth, even if, in the end, I wish them to find their own path." Dave's pedagogical objective, right up to the present time, was to learn how to respect his students' search for meaning without underplaying the value of the wisdom he had gained from his own lifelong search.

As an aside, this, I believe, is the central dilemma for all postmodern educators: How can a teacher find the best balance between freedom and authority? Does a postmodern teacher always have to favor freedom over discipline, the new over the old, or the individual over the group? Can a postmodern teacher have strong moral and political convictions? Can a postmodern teacher be spiritual, or even religious? Can a postmodern educator teach "facts," history, or scientific versions of truth? Is postmodernism something more than a synonym for skepticism, or even nihilism?[6]

In my opinion, Dave's philosophy of education was a rich blend of Buddhist compassion, Taoistic paradox, postmodern irony, a commitment to cultural diversity and religious pluralism, progressive educational principles à là A. S. Neill of the Summerhill School, John Dewey and Paulo Freire, self-exploration, and a respect for civility in all social and educational interactions. His own learnings during the course of his life had been hard-earned and cherished by him. Therefore, he was left with an abiding educational question: How could he construct a usable pedagogy with his students—based on his postmodern discernment of what was considered "normal" and what wasn't—that would be both self-respecting and "other" respecting?

That is, how could he draw upon the authority of his own experience and knowledge in such a way that he didn't unwittingly preempt his students' needs to learn from their own mistakes and successes? This, after all, was the way that Dave had composed his own life story. And he would be the first to say that what was good enough for him should also be good enough for his students.

Dave's strengths were many in his thesis. For one, he told a great story. I read Dave as the central protagonist in his narrative: a compassionate yet committed outsider and innovator who wanted to teach in conventional public school educational systems. But having failed dismally to get a teaching license, he ended up in a private school where he could live an authentic educational life. This narrative presentation of himself as an advocate for school reform was real because Dave was real. He didn't stack the deck in his favor. Also, he used the technique of dialogue expertly. Some writers, like myself, are tone deaf to credible dialogue. Dave was not. His verbal exchanges with students always rang true. He knew how adolescents talked. He knew their cadences, figures of speech, and language tics. He let them speak in their own voices without making them mere mouthpieces for his educational homilies.

Moreover, he employed just the right mix of formal and informal writing in his SPN. This kept his thesis accessible and even fun to read. He was also able to punctuate his philosophical investigations into the strengths and weaknesses of postmodern theory by referring often to both his personal family experiences and his professional work with students and colleagues. Postmodernism was more than an obscure philosophical system to Dave. It was an actual way of being—something to be lived as well as theorized. So it seemed to us, his thesis committee.

Dave's overall forte in writing an SPN, in my opinion, was his ability to blend theory and practice, to artfully combine the abstract and the concrete. One member of his committee, a newly hired assistant professor who previously had her doubts about the "rigor" of SPN writing, told me later that Dave had won her over. She was pleasantly surprised at the depth of scholarly inquiry in Dave's thesis. This colleague and I have become very good friends since Dave's defense. In fact, she is the person whom I refer to as the "public intellectual" in chapter 6. She was not ready to embrace a philosophy of postmodernism—and, I will add, why should she? Nevertheless, my colleague felt that Dave had explained its rudiments with remarkable clarity. This was all that she could ask for.

Moreover, Dave's personal candor was admirable. Not once did he present himself in his SPN as a super crusader for educational reform, always on the right side of goodness, justice, and the progressive way. He overcame the temptation to set up educational heroes and villains. He was more than willing to let his pedagogical warts show in all their unattractiveness. In some ways, he presented himself as a Don Quixote tilting at windmills. He was willing to allow his readers to chuckle at some of his personal foibles. This, by the way, was an excellent strategy for hooking his readers. Show your idiosyncracies, laugh at yourself, and let the reader know that you are human. Hence, you win their sympathy as well as their trust.

In his thesis committee's estimation, Dave was able to put meat on the bare bones of postmodern theory by talking openly and honestly about his life and work as a teacher, and this included his failures and self-doubts. I think it very appropriate that Dave ended his thesis with a short section called "Hey Mom, I found meaning (for now)." The key to understanding Dave's disposition toward his personal and pedagogical life is to foreground the two small words he chose to put in parentheses: "for now." If only more educators, or true believers everywhere, would be willing to do the same. If only I could put this postmodern prompt into practice in my own classroom with more consistency. Thanks to Dave, I will try even harder.

PATTI:
"Composing a Pedagogy of Mattering—
A Scholarly Personal Narrative on What It Means
to Matter in Education"

I have known Patti for the better part of 20 years. I remember her as a young graduate student in the counseling program who just didn't seem to fit the prototype for a school counselor. She was a knowledge seeker by temperament and taste. She loved to read and to write, and she enjoyed the pursuit of learning for its own sake. She was less interested in studying the textbook techniques of counseling than she was in asking the deeper philosophical questions about meaning-making. She was creative, assertive, and verbal. My most vivid image of Patti 20 years ago was of someone who wanted to matter more than anything else. She wanted to be learned and wise so much that it hurt.

She wanted to count for something in the professional and scholarly world. She wanted the world of academia to sit up and take notice of her. She wanted me to give her permission to be a scholar as well as a competent practitioner. Twenty years later, when she was my doctoral student, I was not the least bit surprised when she approached me wanting to do an SPN on "mattering." Once again, that old French saw, *plus ça change, plus c'est la même chose* (the more things change, the more they stay the same), seemed appropriate. The major difference between the

Patti just out of college and the Patti 20 years later, however, was that the more mature Patti wanted to become a scholar on her own terms, not on mine or on anyone else's. One more personal observation about Patti: I believe that today she is a scholar-teacher-administrator-counselor through and through. She has taught me much, and I remain indebted to her. The professor has become the student. This is as it should be, and she would like this.

During that 20-year hiatus when I lost touch with Patti, she had gone on to live a full personal and professional life. She got married and became a parent. Her professional work ranged from counseling in a corrections facility to administering, advising, and teaching in a transition program for students at a local, four-year college. When we reconnected, I found her sitting one semester in my philosophy of education course, testing out whether she might be ready for doctoral study. She was the same old Patti, but with several additional years of practical experience, deeper questions to ask, and a need to explore further the ideas of philosophers and educational theorists.

She took to philosophy of education like a fish takes to water. Philosophy became her natural habitat for one exciting semester. She loved swimming in its waters. She has since told me that her studies that semester awakened her from what Kant once called his "philosophical slumbers." She rediscovered the satisfactions of dwelling for a while in the life of the mind, and being encouraged by me and her classmates to wonder aloud about the meaning of education and her life for three hours every single week, for one full semester.

In my opinion, Patti wrote as fine an SPN doctoral dissertation as any student of mine had up to that point. Her organizing construct was simple and direct: Effective teaching is all about helping students to know that they matter. Her subconstruct was equally simple; namely, that helping students to know they matter does not mean coddling them. There is always a pedagogical moment in teaching when one's personal story needs to intersect with sound scholarship. Good teachers know when and how to exploit these moments.

Good learning is "authentic" learning, both for teachers and for students. Whatever the unique teaching style (and Patti is a gifted lecturer as well as a good one-on-one tutor), educators can help students matter. The best teaching is "relational" teaching. SPN is a mattering technique that students themselves, at secondary and higher education levels, need to learn and use. Good teachers, in Patti's words, know that students ought to be "living part of the content" they are learning.

What exactly is "mattering"? Here, in her dissertation, was Patti's take on this rich concept: "The basic tenet of mattering seems to rest on being acknowledged or noticed as a person." At another place in the dissertation, she remarked, "In the mattering conversation [in the classroom], students need to believe that what they have to say counts." Here is yet another perspective: "In order to matter academically, students must feel that their lives interweave with what they are learning. I believe that in order to feel as if we matter in a class, our thoughts, opinions, interests, and experiences must be incorporated." As a teacher, I can only add "amen" to all of this.

Although, as Patti pointed out, mattering has lately been the subject of a growing body of research, it has gone largely unnoticed by educators in the academy. Why? Because, in my opinion, few scholars have written about it in cogent, everyday English. After examining all the relevant data in her research and practice, Patti was able to offer simple definitions, and practical applications, of mattering that were a drastic improvement on the jargon-loaded studies of others on the same topic. I felt, after reading Patti's work, that mattering did indeed matter, because she made it seem as if mattering mattered *to her*—in every way. She was very careful to approach her narrative on mattering by placing herself at the center of the story; to talk about those times in her own personal and professional life when she felt that she did or did not matter. Never once did Patti write herself out of her mattering narrative by becoming the omniscient, and "objective," philosopher or empirical scientist.

Patti's dissertation was full of wonderful practical suggestions for teachers in helping their students to matter. She recommended the use of reflective journaling, letters, dialogues, "scholarly personal lectures," continuing "teacher development" in building the skills to encourage mattering, "group learning," and "critical reading," among a host of other activities. Each of these recommendations came with her signature "sage advice" (a favorite phrase of Patti's), based on Patti's own classroom teaching and her mastery of the relevant scholarship. In rereading her work today, I am even more impressed with Patti's uncanny ability to shape a usable narrative for teachers by drawing from the growing body of research on mattering, as well as from her own experiences in the classroom. Hers is truly a pedagogy that matters because it is down-to-earth and serviceable; yet it is also an excellent piece of original scholarship.

Patti was a gifted writer and storyteller. She knew well how to play up her strengths in her dissertation. Some of my students who have since read Patti's dissertation have remarked to me that they couldn't put it down. What they were saying to me was that they were "hooked." Patti was a master at knowing how to hook her readers. As I stated in chapter

3, constructs are good, but *constructs*–no matter how clear and brilliant—
without hooks go unread. Patti hooked by becoming vulnerable. Patti
hooked by telling stories. Patti hooked by being honest. Patti hooked by
using her personal stories to deliver the philosophical and pedagogical
payload. A good SPN always puts stories in the service of ideas. This
principle turned out to be Patti's first commandment in doing an SPN.

For example, from the very beginning of her dissertation, Patti told
a series of frankly revealing vignettes about herself. One comes to mind
immediately. Deep into her dissertation, Patti revealed the story of her
continuing, 20-year bout with depression. She talked openly about the
"spiral down" that virtually immobilized her throughout her life. Later
in her adult years, when she became a mother, she sought the services
of a psychiatrist.

Here is what Patti learned about teaching from her sessions with a
therapist, and from "inner dialogues" with herself:

> The greatest benefits of dialogue, both with a therapist and
> with myself, have come from insights into my humanness and
> into my teaching. It is through dialogue that I found the Guru-
> Woman [in me], a little "out there," I know, but nonetheless,
> given my background, she has been life giving. This is the
> part of me that has survived and thrived over the last 40
> years—the mojo rising. Historically, I have been much more
> willing to make room for the critic in my life than for the wise
> one. . . . Writing dialogues is one way to access the sweetheart
> guru-woman and quiet the critic. . . . As I come to better under-
> stand how my internal dialogues play out, I can watch how
> the critics and the sage ones evidenced themselves in my own
> learning and my own teaching. In this way, I can learn from
> the critics, but not allow them to silence or restrain me.

Throughout her dissertation, Patti also added a number of poetic
and metaphoric "interludes." She was a skilled metaphorist, and she
knew how to mine this vein of gold for all it was worth. Her several
interludes included reflections on cooking and bird watching, two of
Patti's beloved avocations. At all times, these interludes connected directly to the more academic points she was attempting to make—about
mattering, and the importance of scholarly personal narrative writing for
both teachers and students. Here are excerpts from one of my favorites,
an interlude she called "Cooking Chicken":

> Anyone who knows me truly well knows that I love to cook.
> . . . I know how to make béarnaise sauce so it doesn't separate,

how to julienne vegetables so they cook uniformly, how to roast a crisp-skin, moist chicken, how to sear a steak with a peppercorn crust, what makes a good quiche. . . . Cooking well is a lot like teaching well. Just as the cook needs to know basic cooking skills, such as preparing sauces, braising, handling pastry dough, so a teacher needs to know the basics. . . . If you know what you are doing, including how to present information clearly, how to begin and facilitate discussion, how to use groups, how to design effective assignments and exams . . . then teaching can be delicious, wonderful, nourishing. Our students' voices and ideas can feed us. . . . There is more to cooking and teaching than just assembling the ingredients, though. . . . You have to put chicken in the oven and add heat to transform it into roast chicken. . . . You must add the heat and energy of your heart to turn pedagogic technique into teaching that matters.

Patti, as I said earlier, was also a captivating storyteller throughout her dissertation. This was but one more tool in her repertoire to hook the reader. In chapter 1, for example, she led off with a short story called "Many Things Matter: Todd and the Grocery Store." Todd had been an inmate at the correctional center where Patti had taught ten years earlier, and she had recently run into him at the local grocery. At this chance meeting, which was awkward, Todd told Patti how much he had changed his life in the intervening ten years. He "no longer drugged or drank." And he had been married over a decade. It was important that he told her all of this, Patti surmised, because she had been the one who had taught him to read and write during his time in prison, which helped him to be able to pass his high school equivalency exam. Here is the lesson that Patti drew from this encounter:

After a couple of days of thinking about the meeting, I realized that Todd had also changed my life. Locked behind iron doors, in what was called the Prison Learning Center, often by myself, with murderers, rapists, child molesters, thieves, drug and gun runners, arsonists, and addicts, I had come to see myself as a teacher. It was there, in the spatial and educational center of the prison, that I came to understand the power and significance of being an educator. . . . I learned that I had the power and privilege to profoundly change lives. . . . I had made a mark on their [convicts'] lives, and they had done the same to mine.

Patti is currently an educator in a culinary institute, both a teacher and an administrator. In some ways, it is her dream job. In other ways, she still has the pedagogical wanderlust, the inclination to move into new teaching and leadership territory. Patti has always been an educational traveler, wanting to bring her gifts to more and more challenging locales. Now that she knows she can write a sustained piece of scholarly work, and do it well, she wants to educate through her writing as well as by teaching. If I know Patti, her time will come to devote her days to her writing. In fact, I believe that her dissertation contains as many wise insights about the art and craft of SPN as any book I know, including the one you are now reading.

In the final section of her dissertation, what she called her "coda," Patti wrote the following:

> My own individual story continues, and as the story journeys forward, I want to remember Natalie Goldberg's advice: "Trust in what you love, continue to do it, and it will take you where you need to go. And don't worry too much about security. You will eventually have a deep security when you begin to do what you want."[7] I know that this is the last paragraph of my dissertation. My heart aches, and I feel a lump in my throat. The writing has been such a wonderful gift—engaging and life giving. Writing bird by bird [a phrase coined by Anne Lamott meaning bit by bit, or word by word], I flew a little farther. My dissertation is a fine launching pad for flying farther. The end is really a beginning. And, mattering matters.

DOUG:
"Reconciling the Life of the Spirit with the Life of an Educational Leader—A Personal Account of 25 Years of Policy Work in the Vermont Department of Education"

I sat with Doug, someone whom I had never met, in my favorite restaurant one late summer morning. His doctoral advisor had recommended me to him, and so he sought me out. His hair was white, and his face unlined. He was 50ish, earnest, and very serious, although he did try to smile occasionally. He seemed to be a little nervous, but not much. I had the strong sense that I was his last resort. He was smooth in making his case to be my SPN student, and I made it a point to listen with my third narrative ear as he told me his doctoral story.

Doug had been in our doctoral program for several years, and was

ABD. A bright man, deputy commisioner of education in my state, well-liked and respected throughout Vermont, Doug had reached what, for him, might have been the end of the doctoral line. He was uninterested in doing either a qualitative or a quantitative dissertation. His advisor told him that he was a great storyteller. Why, then, didn't he consider doing an SPN? Doug was a busy professional educator at the state level, and was close to retirement, having served 25 years at the state department of education. While the doctorate would have been nice, Doug was not willing to sell his soul in order to get it. But he was curious about "this SPN thing."

We moved quickly from small talk to big talk. I explained to him, in gentle yet clear terms, that SPN was more than just writing about himself. Sure, he might be a great storyteller, but, in writing an SPN, the stories must be universalizable. They needed to be a conduit for larger meanings—the means to deliver readers to greater ends. An SPN might not require structured interviews or statistical analyses, but it did call for much proof texting and scholarly referencing. An SPN might not ask writers to do extensive ethnographic research, but it did demand that they be willing to do in-depth self-inquiry.

Moreover, an SPN enjoined writers to do extensive background reading along with much ongoing self-reflection. Most important, though, an SPN obliged writers to leave the technical jargon, and the conventional research writing models, behind. Instead, it urged them to find a unique writing style that best captured their genuine voices. My shortcut message to Doug was this: An SPN is not easy. In fact, it would be the toughest writing he would ever do in his life. Doug, I might add, went on to get the message perfectly. To quote his dissertation: "Robert's course in writing scholarly personal narratives was without doubt the best and the most rigorous course I've taken in my academic career."

After we finished our breakfast conversation, I encouraged Doug to take my SPN course, but I did have some reservations. I wondered, for example, if a career educational bureaucrat could write something other than a memorandum or a policy statement. Would Doug be willing to reach beyond his public leader persona in order to explore both the dark and the bright sides of his educational story, and chance going public in a dissertation with his results? What did Doug actually profess by way of values about his work, if anything? Was he authentic? He seemed so professionally unflappable and self-confident.

Would the carefully guarded, diplomatic, public Doug ever let his guard down? Was this a guy who would come clean, be honest, and tell his story regardless of where the chips might fall? Moreover, did he have enough mastery of the relevant literature to deepen and enrich his story intellectually? I discovered later, much to my embarrassment, that what I was doing at that breakfast meeting was reducing Doug to a cardboard figure right out of my convenient little laboratory of educational-administrator stereotypes. As I got to know him, Doug turned out to be exactly the opposite of all my worst impressions of statewide educational leaders.

However, it did take a while for Doug to get into the SPN flow once he got in my seminar. At first, he didn't have a specific set of constructs to guide his thinking about his dissertation. He wasn't sure how to hook readers. He wasn't sure how to tell macro- or microstories in such a way as to advance more general themes and convictions. He did have a vague idea that he wanted to write about his quarter of a century as an educational policy maker in Vermont. Unfortunately, Doug's first set of SPN papers read like official state department dicta. Frankly, I found them lifeless in style and substance. I think he did, too. They seemed to be slightly revised reiterations of work that he had done in his previous policy-related coursework. My feedback to him was disconcerting: "You don't quite get the point of SPN writing. You need to write more from the heart and less from the head." Then, I asked him: "Doug, what do you *really feel strongly about?*"

Finally, in one of his papers, almost as a throwaway, Doug revealed that he came from several generations of ordained Baptist ministers. His dad, also a minister, and now deceased, had been his role model and hero. Moreover, Doug had graduated from a biblically based, evangelical college. Doug's gentle revelation was buried in the middle of a recounting of several policy initiatives he had taken as a deputy commissioner of education. But the revelation stood out for me because there seemed to be a different tone in that paragraph; perhaps some personal yearning unfulfilled, some regret previously undeclared. I also knew from many years of experience that students in my writing course don't usually stumble into accidental self-disclosures. There are no throwaways for SPN writers. All self-revelations, at some level of consciousness, are calculated. As existentialists are prone to say, there are no accidents.

I followed up on this revealing bit of religious information, and began to ask Doug some pointed, but respectful, questions. This was an easy thing for me to do because I have studied, taught, and written about religion and spirituality for many years. All my students were aware of this, including Doug. I believe he knew exactly what he was doing when he wrote about his family's religious past; it was almost as if he were waiting to see what I would do with his disclosure. In that one paragraph, whether he knew it or not, Doug had discovered the main construct, story, and hook for his dissertation. From that point on, Doug, the dissertation, and I were off and rolling. Everything fell into place.

Here is the biblical proof text that provided the source for Doug's central construct: "No man can serve two masters; for either he will hate the one, and love the other; or else he will hold on to the one, and despise the other. Ye cannot serve God and mammon." Here is Doug's exegesis of that passage from Matthew 6:24:

> The Bible is clear in its teaching that we cannot truly serve two masters. . . . To me that passage strikes even closer when it is interpreted in the inverse—every man must serve one master with all of his heart and all of his being. . . . As I have stated in many different ways in this dissertation, I have decided to define my life and the way I live it around my faith and trust in God through Jesus Christ. I believe that I can be an ambassador for Christ, as the Bible directs me to be, and still be an effective, loyal employee of the Vermont Department of Education.

Doug's central construct, triggered by Matthew's biblical verse, was that it was indeed possible to live as an evangelical Christian and still find common ground between one's profound religious beliefs and one's work as a secular educator. If his own career was any indication, evangelical Christians could serve two masters without becoming spiritually and professionally schizophrenic, or so compromised as to end up morally bankrupt.

What was so powerful about Doug's extensive examination of the many policy conflicts between church and state that he faced during his long career was his uncanny ability to narrate a number of nonjudgmental, parable-like stories. Trained to be a journalist in college, Doug knew well how to tell a story in simple, direct language, without once diminishing the complexity of an idea. Also, during his many years of work as a toastmaster and presenter for the state department of education, Doug knew how to let his stories do the talking, as well as the teaching. Like his divine hero, Jesus, Doug preferred to make his points less by pontificating and more by narrating.

In his dissertation, Doug's Christian message of love, compassion, and forgiveness never came across as dogmatic or proselytizing. Again, like his divine mentor, Doug let his deeds convey the depth of his commitment to his Christian beliefs. After reading his dissertation, one member of the faculty, who had known Doug previously, remarked to me that Doug was one of the most "morally decent" human beings she had ever known in the profession. The surprise for her was that Doug was an evangelical Christian. Not once in 20 years had Doug let on to her that he was a devout Christian. Yet my colleague was not the least bit surprised by Doug's disclosures because, ex post facto, Doug's life now appeared to add up. "Of course, Doug is a Christian," my colleague said to me. "The way that he treats others is always above and beyond the call of official duty. It all makes sense."

One hook for the reader in Doug's dissertation was his complete willingness to be honest with himself and his readers; to admit openly his career-long ambivalence about trying to be both a state servant and a Christian servant. It was not always smooth sailing for him to keep the two personae in harmony in his job. In fact, I read much of Doug's dissertation as a thinly veiled statement of remorse about those times he felt he had failed to live up to his Christian beliefs. So often he wanted to speak out publicly in behalf of his Christian convictions, but something always held him back. I sensed sadness as he recounted his personal stories of compromise, self-doubt, and unwillingness to offend his colleagues.

Two stories among several stood out. Doug once attended an educational conference at a local college. Doug writes, "I had spent the entire drive from Montpelier [to the conference] thinking about missed opportunities to tell others about my faith and again prayerfully asking God for another chance." After the keynote speaker's opening comments, he invited members of the audience to "turn to the person sitting next to them and tell them about the thing that caused the most significant change in your life." Doug had braced himself for this moment, having gone over in his mind what he would say to his colleague from the state board of education sitting next to him about the profound, life-changing impact that Christianity had on his life.

> As I looked at her, my mind was flooded with the thoughts of my morning devotional and prayer time. Be ready always to give an answer. . . . I am not ashamed of the gospel of Jesus Christ. . . . The single most life-changing thing that ever happened to me. . . . Turn to the person next to you and tell them. . . . Lord, give me another chance. . . .

Unfortunately, Doug never did get to tell his Christian story, as he was interrupted by a message to take an important phone call from the commissioner of education. "As I stepped out of the row of seats to the aisle, I felt relieved, but I hadn't gone more than two steps before I was immersed in guilt. Once again I had dodged the opportunity to share my faith." During the entire day, Doug tortured himself about taking that phone call and thereby choosing not to tell his story. He wanted to find a way to engage his colleague in conversation in order to tell that story, but he didn't. That night during prayer, Doug "recommitted myself to the challenge and asked for help as I faced this difficult obligation to bear witness to my Savior."

The opportunity came another time. It was as if his prayers had been answered. Doug appeared before the Vermont legislature during the 2002 session as an expert witness from the state department of education. The controversial issue was teaching about homosexuality in the public schools. This was a hot topic because Vermont had been the first state to legalize civil unions. As a result, there were hard feelings throughout the state among some Christian and Republican conservatives who felt sold out by the state judiciary, the liberal governor, and the legislature. Here was Doug's statement of ambivalence about the topic:

> I have always tried to resolve my feelings and beliefs about
> homosexuality and how it should be viewed and addressed in
> our schools and in our society. . . . I believe that the Bible
> clearly states that homosexuality is an abomination in God's
> eyes. . . . there is no doubt that homosexual behavior is a sin.
> So how do I reconcile this with God's love and desire for
> everyone?

So, here Doug sat, before the congressional committee, religiously opposed to homosexual behavior, believing that, just as *he* needed to live a disciplined lifestyle due to his life-threatening, Type 1 diabetes, so, too, those who are homosexually inclined had to practice self-discipline in order to overcome their disordered sexual desires. On the other hand, though, Doug had gay friends and colleagues whom he had come to respect and admire. Moreover, he was at that committee hearing as a representative of the state department and not of his church. Now what? How would it ever be possible to take a position one way or another on a bill introduced by a Republican legislator to prohibit all references to homosexuality in public schools without having to compromise something precious to himself in either case?

With every eye in the congressional room on him, Doug sought the wise middle way. He presented the state department's position that the local school board, and not the state, should make curricular decisions for the public schools. But he also went one step further: he told a personal story about his son. During a health education class in his son's public school classroom, the teacher invited a Planned Parenthood visitor to talk about sexually transmitted diseases. The hands-on presentation on condoms was embarrassing and offensive to both Doug's son, and to Doug and his wife. Doug told the committee how later he, and a small group of parents, met with the principal, aired their concerns, and he felt truly heard. The message he delivered was that these types of presentations, no matter how well-intended, could end up offending devout Christian children and parents. The congressional committee listened carefully to Doug's testimony, understood his point, and thanked him "for helping the committee understand how state and local curriculum policies worked together." Here is Doug's take on his testimony:

> The discussion of this one incident only took about five minutes of the entire session with the committee that afternoon. I didn't get to the point of sharing the details of my beliefs and my spiritual faith, nor did I reveal my Biblically-based views on homosexuality. But I did feel positively that I had tried to help those in the room see some possible middle ground between state mandated policy and the responsibility of the local school system to work with parents, teachers, and others in the community to respect the beliefs of parents and to do what is right.

Doug's entire dissertation dealt with this "apparent dichotomy" of how to live a life of religious integrity while being asked to serve two masters. His many candid stories brought the problem to light from several angles. They also led to a series of concrete recommendations for Christians, indeed for anyone with strong personal beliefs, who might someday find themselves working in the public policy arena. In addition to his policy proposals, Doug's dissertation was filled with numerous references to relevant readings and quotations. His bibliography alone contained more than 100 scholarly entries.

Doug ended his dissertation with a series of brief "letters from the heart," written for people who had played a pivotal role in his life. I was honored that he wrote a letter to me, a secular humanist and atheist, and someone who had known him for only a year. But I was particularly touched by his letter to his deceased dad. He ended that letter with these words: "I know we will meet someday again in the presence of the Lord in that place where questions and answers become one. Until then I will continue, with clear purpose, to become the man you meant me to be."

Every single person on Doug's dissertation committee was moved by this final, powerful, personal sentiment. One member whispered the following to me after Doug finished making a presentation for the benefit of so many of his colleagues and friends (including his minister) who had come to his dissertation defense: "Did you read Doug's letter to his dad? I never met his dad, but based on what I know about Doug, his father must have been quite a man. And if his dad does still 'live' somewhere in an afterlife, I'll bet a month's salary that he's pretty proud of the way that Doug turned out." I could only nod in agreement, and enjoy even more Doug's public moment of spiritual self-exposure. He had, indeed, come out . . . as a Christian. I am here to testify that not a single person in his audience fainted in shock or erupted in fury. To the contrary, those who knew him loved and respected him even more. I know that I did.

LOU:
"Preparing Holistic Educational Leaders through the Use of Instructional Narrative— A Personal Account of One Principal's Leadership Persona"

I was a little nervous as I sat next to my colleague who was ready to introduce me to her dissertation proposal writing class. Ten people were waiting expectantly to hear me talk about SPN, and what a proposal might look like in this genre. Because I usually experience some performance jitters whenever I do a guest shot for a colleague, especially when I don't know anyone in the class, I try to pick out a friendly face and make full eye contact. It was easy for me to do this with Lou who was sitting on the left side of the classroom facing me. He was probably in his mid-40s, brawny, dark-skinned, with a full head of black hair, and a very animated face. Most of all, he welcomed me immediately with his warm smile, and later with his kind and supportive words. I knew from the outset that I would like this man.

During my presentation, he nodded frequently. His eyes sparkled with enthusiasm. He reacted in all the right places to my laugh lines. His questions, and responses, were enclosed in fascinating mini-narratives that he told about himself, his school, his colleagues, and his family. He spoke to me by using vivid philosophical analogies that I recognized immediately. I learned later that Lou had been a philosophy major as an undergraduate. When I heard that, I knew that we would click intellectually. We were kindred spirits, although his Platonic and Thomistic worldviews were very different from mine. Nevertheless, we were asking similar questions about knowledge and values.

Lou was also a practicing Catholic. Later in our relationship, he would call me "Nash, the Agnostic" (this is the way he referred to me throughout his dissertation, even though I am an atheist). I tagged him "Lou, the Believer." This was all in good fun, because Lou was fun. He was wonderful to be around, and he still is. Lou is a Renaissance man, a man for all seasons, with a sense of humor accompanied by a robust hug. But he also had a serious, reflective side that came out in his dissertation.

I learned that day in class that Lou was a Vermont elementary school principal, that he was on the fast track in his doctoral program, that he traveled a great distance to get to the university each week, and that he loved to read the classics. He also revered the Italian language; in fact, he loved everything Italian. As we got to know each other very well during the next year, he would often counter my use of Latin phrases with his Italian phrases. He spoke fluent Italian, a living language. I wrote fluent Latin, a dead language. He was Italian. I was Irish. He loved Italian food; I loved it even more, I think. This was another point of contact between us that became important. It led eventually to shared lunches at Pizzeria Uno where we discussed the pressing educational questions of the day, and where I did some dissertation advising between bites of a deep-dish, four-cheese pizza.

Here's a brief personal aside of my own that I think is relevant to my relationship with Lou: In Boston, where I grew up, the Italians would frequently beat up the Irish, just for the hell of it. The opposite was also true. To this day, I remember an Italian nun, Sister Francesca, who was my teacher in a Catholic elementary school, St. Gregory's, in Boston. She did not like me one bit. At least twice a week, she would make some disparaging comment about me in front of my peers; about my Irish heritage, about how there were just too many priests who were Irish, about my dad who was an Irish cop, and about my parents who were "unbaptized" and didn't go to church. I feared and hated her because she made a fool out of me.

After I got to know Lou, I thought again of this Italian nun. She would have learned a lot from Lou, the Italian Believer, who turned out to be one of the kindest, gentlest, and wisest students I ever had. This is the way I would introduce them to one another today, if Sister Francesca were alive: "Sister Francesca, meet Lou, a countryman of yours. Lou, meet Sister Francesca, someone who frightened me to death every single day that I went to school as an eight-year-old. Sister Francesca, please shadow Lou in his role as an elementary school principal for a while, and then do as he does. You'll be a better person, and Christian, because of it, and I won't be afraid of you anymore." I just can't imagine Lou frightening anyone or treating anyone unkindly. I learned later from his course instructor that everyone, including her, in his doctoral cohort felt the same way. Lou was, and is, all about connection and authenticity, the two major organizing themes of this chapter.

Lou's dissertation was construct- and story-rich. His major, organizing construct (it took him a while to come up with one, because Lou is virtually an encyclopedia of information that is not yet alphabetized) was that three qualities are essential for leaders to be effective in public education: pathos, ethos, and spiritus (compassion, morality, and spirituality). Another important construct was his belief that "instructional narratives" could be a powerful tool for training "holistic educational leaders." Lou presented these, and other secondary constructs, from within his personal story where "family, faith, and fate" were so crucial to his own development. Moreover, he created the dramatic structure for his narrative by examining a number of "critical incidents" in his own life.

Not least, Lou took advantage of his vast store of background knowledge in the humanities, leadership theory, and pedagogy in order to enrich and deepen the personal insights in his stories. His scholarly references were profuse and pertinent at all times. But they never intimidated the reader. I found that reading Lou's dissertation was similar to meeting at a coffee shop in downtown Burlington in order to have a serious discussion with bright, down-to-earth folks about many of life's most basic, existential issues.

Moreover, Lou managed to come up with a fresh understanding of SPN that the committee, including myself, found to be very helpful. Here is how he reframed several conversations he and I had had about SPN both in, and outside of, class:

> I remember the conversations and remember the sense of what [Robert] was saying. . . . In weaving a scholarly personal narrative, you, the writer, must sustain the personal thread, the narrative thread (the telamon [a buttressing structure] of the tale which supports your life's story), and the thematic thread (the construct of the story, the universal understanding, telling truths, or insightful intuitions). When the writer is willing to be honest about content, reflective about its meaning, and concerned about its implications for others, a good story is being told.

Throughout his dissertation, Lou drew on the interdisciplinary wisdom of thinkers representing such fields as philosophy, religion, the classics, leadership theory, and pedagogy. And oh yes, he also managed to display his mastery of several languages throughout his manuscript, including Latin and Italian. For example, his dissertation's dedication to his wife included the words *amo, ergo sum* (I love, therefore I am) and *je t'adore* (I adore you). His dedication to his daughter read *sapere audi* (dare to be wise). And this was just for starters.

What would you do, for example, with this Italian passage, that showed up as early as page six of his dissertation: *"buona fortuna, cara amica. Auguri a tutti chi vivando con il cuore! Vi voglio sai . . ."*? My Latin helped, but not much. Knowing Lou, but not knowing Italian, the committee was sure that this was a very friendly greeting sent our way to get us positioned to read his dissertation in the right frame of mind. How could it be otherwise? Wasn't this Lou, after all, charming us with the most romantic of romance languages?

Nonetheless, the main hook in Lou's work was the story, always the story. His many tales pulled us in; they seduced us. They were the vehicle that delivered all the lessons he learned, the love and respect he showed to everyone he knew, the leadership he manifested, and the compassion and passion he lived every single day of his life. One story in particular, the story of Lou's confrontation with his own mortality and finitude, was the most trenchant hook of all.

If, as storytellers, Socrates was the "seditious" gadfly who died for his "crimes" against the state, and Nietzsche the angry values provocateur who died a lonely, syphilitic madman, then Lou was the seductive and gentle storyteller who was also a survivor. He told the story of his Italian background, the roots of which went back many generations in Italy. He talked about how the virtues of compassion, morality, and spirituality had been bred into him by his Italian ancestors. He narrated the story of how he was awakened one night to learn that one of his staff members at school was killed by her husband in the middle of a drunken argument.

He revealed that he suffered from a life-threatening, deteriorating condition called cardiomyopathy. In time, Lou will need a heart transplant or he will die. As he pointed out in his dissertation, he lives medically as an ABD prospect (not "all but dissertation," but "all but dead"). The optimistic and ever hopeful Lou, though, has since reframed this to mean "always being determined." He talked about the profoundly spiritual, déjà vu experience he had when his beloved grandfather died. He described the time when he and his wife learned that their precious, only daughter was diagnosed with an incurable condition called Crohn's Disease. She would survive, but she would have to find a way to deal with this enervating disease for the rest of her life. He talked about the death of his mother from a "major cardiac event," wondering, perhaps, if this would also be his fate someday. He also mentioned his brother's struggle with a similar, very serious cardiac condition, and the major surgery it required.

Lou narrated all of his personal stories within the context of his commitment to family, faith, and fate, as well as within the personal story of his lifelong attempt to practice the virtues of compassion, morality, and spirituality. This sixfold structure provided a cohesive framework for his stories. Here is how he summed up his contextual-personal structure:

> Is there . . . some greater entity? Who is to say? Certainly not me. I know there is purpose in my life, and it seems that fate enables me to consider that purpose through my life's experiences. Although each of us may have a different set of circumstances to tell our stories, there is a universality in the telling of the story. Fate helps outline the story that each of us fleshes out through narrativization. Faith helps to give the story meaning. And family provides the context for the story.

The applied, professional section of Lou's dissertation was as good as any I've seen yet in SPN writing. Lou spent some time describing how he first got involved in education. His stories about his teaching and administering, from when he first started to where he is now, were humorous and serious at the same time. It was obvious to me, and to his committee, that Lou was devoted to his work. Indeed, the word "devoted" may be too weak to describe the passionate attachment he has had to his work as an educator. Let me say that Lou was, and still is, "in love with" his work. According to Lou, his current work as a principal in a small Vermont rural community represented the love of his life, surpassed only by the love that he had for his family. It was clear to everyone on his committee that in his work as an administrator, Lou embodied all the meanings of the word "principal": someone who was both leader and teacher, follower and learner, lover and loved.

The most innovative section of Lou's dissertation, at least for me, was the framework he developed for using scholarly (Lou also used the term "instructional") personal narrative as a tool for professional development. Why was SPN important for future educational leaders to practice? According to Lou:

> Scholarly personal narrative plays an integral role in the professional development process for present and future holistic educational leaders. . . . narrativizing those ["aha"] moments

where intuition and imagination conjoin with our skills and techniques, and sharing them with others, heightens our own self-awareness and the level of awareness in others. Using the method of scholarly personal narrative as instructional narrative, we inhale the air surrounding us and exhale the intoxication of inspiration which has grown within.

Building on the postmodern assumptions regarding SPN that I describe in chapter 2, what he called "Nashtonics," Lou presented a step-by-step program for developing "leadership personae in educational administrators." His program included the following activities: reflective practice, support groups, narrative therapy, study groups, journal writing, writers' workshops, leadership development institutes, formal coursework, clinical supervision, and mentoring. Once again, all of these practical implications grew out of Lou's personal stories as an educator, parent, husband, son, and as someone struggling with the life-and-death implications of his degenerative heart disease.

Lou closed his dissertation with an inventive "epilogue," in which he reverted to his story-telling style. He told a series of "stories of fictional characters based on actual events," with himself as the nonfictional, primary protagonist. One of the events was the response of a school principal to 9/11 as he was visiting the actual site of ground zero. Another was the story of how "heart wrenching" it can be for the parents, the school, and the community whenever a student dies. In his closing section, Lou also scripted a conversation about scholarly personal narrative learnings, what he called a "multilogue," among a fictional narrator, principal, aspiring educational leader, superintendent, department of education official, university academician, legislator, and governor.

All of these creative tools allowed Lou to summarize and conclude his dissertation in his characteristically dramatic fashion. What follows is one of Lou's more dramatic, and moving, self-disclosures:

> My perspective has been shaped by my medical situation, and the realization that I am truly mortal. My style takes shape through the various experiences rooted in the beliefs I hold dearly, molded by my three musketeers—pathos, ethos, and spiritus, and my personal trinity of family, faith, and fate. No matter what, the reality is mine. Truth be known, it is my story which I have never shared in its entirety with anyone else before. That is, before now and before you, dear reader and leader. It is my treasure store which I give unto you. It is

not a special story, but it is certainly mine. . . . You, too, have the capability to tell your story—through scholarly personal narrative, and instructional narrative is the tool or technique which can assist.

And then the day arrived for Lou's defense. We sat in a room around a table. There would be no powerpoint presentation here. Lou's leadership persona didn't include powerpoint, at least not on that day. Present in the room were teachers from Lou's school, other doctoral students, his wife, friends, and the faculty. We on the committee were each given a passage to read from Lou's dissertation. He started the proceedings with a nonverbal warmup exercise that involved every single person in the room. This was one of the exercises that Lou's teachers used each day in their own classroom morning circles to bond students and teachers alike for the rest of the day.

After loosening us up with this activity, an activity that few of us awkward, verbal, faculty types got right, Lou began to talk about his life journey as it related to his dissertation. On his cue, at strategic places during his presentation, each of us then read an excerpt from Lou's dissertation in order to add conceptual muscle to his life story. In this way, we who were sitting around that table were as much a part of Lou's dissertation story as he was, at least for a couple of hours. More important to us educators, though, Lou was actually modeling the virtues of authenticity and connection that were such a central feature of his dissertation and his leadership style. This was as much about us as it was about him.

In this austere academic setting, a stuffy Phi Beta Kappa room with at least three-quarters of a century of history, Lou was trying to make the venue more learner-friendly by creating his own dissertation-defense story. It worked. I rarely had so much fun, or been challenged so much intellectually, or felt closer to my colleagues, during a dissertation defense than on that day. We faculty soon realized that we weren't there to parade our intellectual prowess, or to interrogate a doctoral student so that he could demonstrate his right to enter the ranks of the intellectual elite. Lou would have none of this, and I was glad. For him connection was everything. Without it, learning is severely diminished in the classroom, whether at the elementary or at the doctoral levels.

In the root sense of the word, we were all *scholars* that day, "playing" with one another, as well as playing with Lou—his ideas, his stories, and his philosophies of life and learning. Lou was also being the *principal* in every sense of the word that I alluded to earlier. And we were being *students*, in the root sense of the word: According to the Oxford English Dictionary, the Latin *studere* connotes much more than merely being engaged in serious, formal study. It also means being a zealous and enthusiastic seeker of knowledge. Further, it connotes being in doubt, being perplexed, asking questions, and looking for resolution. It suggests paying regard to the possibility that something valuable will show up during the quest to know. It also suggests exercising the emotions as well as the intellect in order to know. Finally, it means being responsive to people's feelings and personal welfare as well as to their ideas.

On that day, we were doing all of this and more, thanks to Lou's leadership. *We were the teachers and we were the taught; we were the knowers and we were the seekers.*[8] As his committee agreed on later, Lou's dissertation could be read as an extended commentary on the deeper meaning of these words. Our parting words to Lou were: *Buona fortuna. Amici sempre.* We wished him good health, good work, good love, and good play, all the conditions that Freud believed were necessary for living a full and happy life.

Conclusion: Authenticity and Connection

The need to be an authentic educator, true to oneself above all else, often comes into conflict with the practical need to compromise in order to bring about a greater good. Similarly, the need to go it alone as a professional is often contrary to the need to find connection for support and sustenance. Each of the four authors in this chapter, in their own narrative fashions, are attempting to reconcile these opposing needs, because they believe that reconciliation is both possible and desirable. They look for complementarity, and they want to resolve contradictions.

Dave, the postmodern educator, positions himself in his educational narrative as the crusading outsider. He wants to construct and teach the truth on his, not the system's, terms. Yet he also knows that unless he is willing to make reasonable compromises in his private school, then no one's needs will be fully served. Dave's challenge in the years to come will be to continue his authentic struggle against insensitive bureaucracies and arbitrary authorities in education without encouraging his students to become iconoclasts. How Dave resolves these, and other, dichotomies in his own everyday behavior will speak volumes to his students and colleagues. He did this superbly in my courses, and so I'm confident that he can do this equally well in his life and work.

Patti is the educator who wants her students to know that above all they matter. She has been so successful as a professional because her students feel genuinely listened to and responded to. She knows their names, both literally and figuratively. Patti is also learning that the quest for authenticity in her work must go hand in hand with the ability to connect with others, in addition to her students. She will also have to remind herself over and over again that she, too, matters. Mohammed Ali, the former heavyweight boxing champion, once said that he could sum up his lifelong learnings in three words: "I, you, we." In my opinion, the implications of Ali's mantra for educators are as follows: Find the *I* of yourself first, because this is the prerequisite for finding everything else. Then focus on the *you*, your storytelling students. Finally, find the point of intersection between the *I* and the *you*, and this becomes the *we*. Because, in the end, teaching that matters is not just about me or you. It's about *us*. The reason that Patti has been such a fine educator is because she has "written the book" on the *I-you-we* triad in teaching.

Doug, the believing Christian and state department official, has spent a quarter of a century trying to serve two masters equally. But one master, the state, never got to know the other master, his lord and savior, Jesus Christ. Doug's decision to go public about his Christianity came during his dissertation defense. It was a dramatic moment for him, for me, and for all of his dear friends in the room that day. Finally, he was able to witness his religious beliefs in a public forum. He became fully authentic. Doug's continuing task ahead, in his new position as a program evaluator in an educational think tank in Washington D.C., will be to allow his Christian story to become coextensive with his educator's story. How to do this in a way that will connect him to all of his constituents without setting himself apart from those who hold different beliefs will be his greatest challenge in the years ahead. I have no doubt that Doug will succeed. Ironically, for Doug, one of the insights that the gay rights movement has given him is that to come out of the closet once is to come out of the closet forever. Rarely does one return. Doug will never closet himself again.

Lou, the school principal living with a serious heart condition that could someday kill him, has become a bonhomie and a bon vivant because of it. Lou's direct encounter with his finitude and mortality has intensified his lust for life, love, and learning. He comes across as a real person because his time is too precious to live a lie. Lou seeks connection because he knows that without the support of a community, he is cut off from the very people he needs and who need him. Lou's task as an educator is to continue living his life with passion and compassion, and spreading these qualities to those around him—colleagues, students, and parents alike. Lou's challenge is never to lose hope; to seize life by the jugular and never let go. By telling his wonderful stories in an SPN, and by evoking similar stories from others via their SPNs, Lou will find a way to maintain those lifelines that, whatever the future brings, will sustain him *and* them. Lou is a principal for all seasons and for all reasons.

Epilogue

The SPNs you've been reading about in the last two chapters are still works in progress, even though all the defenses have been successful, and all the degrees have been awarded. No single SPN is perfect, ever. Some writers in these two chapters are more talented by way of craft, some by art, some by construct, some by hook, some by narrative structure, some by scholarship, some by universalized themes, and some by creative use of language. But, no matter how talented the writer, each and every SPN can always be tweaked some more. So, too, can any type of dissertation or thesis, published article or course essay, monograph or book. SPN writers are always polishing and always recrafting; always adding and always subtracting. They do this, I think, because they agree with James Dickey's statement, one of the epigraphs of chapter 3. To make their writing look spontaneous and creative, they need to draft and redraft, and then redraft some more.

Of the SPN writers I've dealt with in these last two chapters, Lou, is preparing a book based on his dissertation. Another writer, Patti, has already developed a series of articles, growing out of her dissertation, that she is submitting to journals for review. Doug has sent his dissertation to one of the most popular Christian writers in the country for feedback, with the ultimate goal of publication. Joe is thinking of basing his future dissertation on his SPN thesis. These writers know that there is always more work to be done, more ideas to develop, more generalizations to make, more stories to tell, and more sources to study and cite.

I will mention here, in passing, several more SPNs that students have written under my supervision. I do this so that you will get an idea of the wide range of possible topics and perspectives that SPN writing offers. Kathy, an adult educator in a small rural Vermont community, and someone who returned to school late in her own life, titled her thesis "Self-Esteem and Women as Learners: An Adult Educator's Personal Journey." George, the best varsity runner in the history of my university, and a history teacher, wrote his thesis on "The Trial of Miles: Approaching Life through Running, Sport, and Education." Jeff, a high-level university administrator, and also a religious seeker, wrote a thesis about his yearlong sabbatical in Israel: "Searching for Myself Under Fire in a

Middle East War Zone: One Educator's Perspective on a Meaningful Form of Pluralism."

Gary, the youngest chief of police in the United States, currently serving in this capacity at my university, wrote a dissertation called "Exploring Education and Leadership: A Police Chief's Personal Journey of Convergence." Jake, a Chicano higher education administrator, is finishing up a dissertation entitled "Marginalized Narratives in the Academy: One Chicano's Attempt to Re-Narrate His Journey in American Higher Education." Elaine, a school principal, and a person with the reputation of being the best math teacher in the state of Vermont, is writing a dissertation called "One Educator's Spiritual Journey through the Garden of Mathematics: Fostering a Passion for Growth and Learning in Public Schools." There are others, but I think you get the idea by now.

CHAPTER SIX

Writing Ourselves as Educators and Scholars: Controversies and Challenges

What are the ethical questions involved when we disclose others' secrets in the act of disclosing our own? . . . Because our own lives never stand free of the lives of others, we are faced with our responsibility to those others whenever we write about ourselves.
—John Paul Eakin, *How Our Lives
Become Stories: Making Selves*

To Virginia Woolf, fact was not necessarly the same as truth. . . . We are not imagined. Our past is real, but it is not static. Can we change the past? No. But we can change how it is remembered because we grow, change, and learn from our experiences.
—Peter M. Ives, "The Whole Truth"

Certain forms of discourse and language are privileged in the academy: the expository essay is valued over the exploratory; the argumentative essay set above the autobiographical; the clear evocation of a thesis preferred to a more organic exploration of a topic; the impersonal, rational voice ranked more highly than the intimate, subjective one. . . . we need to unravel the system that perpetuates these genre dichotomies in order to teach and write the full range of possible genres.
—Gesa E. Kirsch, *Women Writing the Academy:
Audience, Authority, and Transformation*

Passion, Resilience, and Faith

As you probably guessed by now, it's not always smooth sailing for SPN writers in the academy. In fact, the waters of traditional academia can be unusually rough and dangerous for scholarly transgressors to test. There are many obstacles to face, but none, I believe, is insurmountable. I have learned much about writing, teaching, and learning these last half-dozen years in my SPN seminars, but one lesson stands out above all the others. My students have taught me that the three most important qualities needed to stay the course in doing SPN writing are passion, resilience, and faith. So many of my SPN students, at the graduate level especially, have become adept at turning challenge into opportunity, and risk into benefit, because they possess these three qualities.

Passion for doing an SPN is about the excitement and enthusiasm that students often manifest as love and affection for their projects. Resilience points to my students' ability to recover from the inevitable setbacks they face with renewed vigor, spirit, and good humor. And faith has to do with my students' trust that the SPN project is a good thing, and that they possess the constancy necessary to sustain their commitment, particularly when their allegiance to the task becomes onerous. All of the writers of the SPNs in the previous two chapters possessed these three qualities.

In this last chapter, I will talk about some controversies and challenges, and some roadblocks, that I believe are unavoidable for all SPN writers, including students, educators, and university faculty. These roadblocks and challenges put the three above-mentioned qualities to the test. I will group these issues under three section headings: ethics, truth, and politics. Think of what follows as a gentle call to action. Also, think of what follows as written on erasable paper rather than chiseled onto stone tablets. Finally, think of what follows as a gift I freely give to each of you based on what I have learned from teaching my SPN seminars for many years. There are no strings attached to this gift. And I will not be hurt if you decide to return it to the gift giver because it doesn't seem relevant to your specific SPN needs at this time. Think, then, of what I say in this final chapter as my book's denouement without a final resolution. Forgive me one last (I promise) Latin sentence: *mors ianua vitae*: "the end is just the beginning."

Ethics: Do We Own Our Own Lives?

One of my students stopped all of us in our tracks during the final meeting of the first SPN course I ever taught. She asked, "Shouldn't we have a code of ethics for SPN writing? It seems to me that, without one, the possibilities for moral mischief abound." I was embarrassed. Here I'd taught applied ethics courses for years, and yet I never once took the time to examine significant moral issues around SPN writing. Did I just take for granted that we would not misuse the genre? Why didn't students mention some of the ethical dilemmas they were facing in their writing during the term?

In some ways, these dilemmas were inevitable. Hovering over our work that semester were the ubiquitous ethical questions involving privacy, informed consent, intimidation, abuses of power, conscious distortion, lying, self-deception, settling old scores, selective memory, and exploitation, among a host of other dilemmas. Why were my, and their, ethical antennae down? Didn't we already know enough about these ethical pitfalls from reading qualitative researchers and ethnographers who had tried to construct a number of procedural safeguards to deal with these issues?

And so I asked them: Why didn't this question about ethics come up earlier in the semester? After a heated discussion, we decided that because SPN was mainly about the self of the writer, we hadn't even considered the possibility that others could be harmed by SPN writing. It was at this point that the same student asked another question: "Does any one of us completely own our own, personal life?" Once again, our conversation stalled. What could the question possibly mean? Of course, we own our lives. Aren't we autonomous beings, independent agents in the world? Aren't we responsible for ourselves? Don't we have a right to tell our own stories in our own best way? After all, aren't we the ones who are living them?

Perhaps not, as Paul John Eakin asserts in the epigraph at the beginning of this chapter: "Because our own lives never stand free of the lives of others, we are faced with our responsibility to those others whenever we write about ourselves." Eakin has undertaken what I believe is the most in-depth analysis of privacy rights in the literature on what he calls the "ethics of life writing." In this section, I want to look briefly at some SPN privacy issues, as well as the dangers of exploiting others, either consciously or unconsciously, for our own ends. I recommend Eakin's wonderful book, *How Our Lives Become Stories: Making Selves*, for those of you who might want to delve more deeply into the complex ethical issues surrounding privacy rights in SPN writing.[1]

I have three general ethical rules I follow in my own SPN work regarding privacy. First, a person's right to privacy in my writing is nearly inviolable, except when my infringing this right might prevent harm to the person, or to others who exist within the direct orbit of that person. Second, following Kant, I try always to treat each human being as an autonomous end rather than as a means to my end. In other words, I refuse to use another person merely to serve my own SPN purposes.

And third, in spite of these first two principles, I do not believe that the right to privacy is an ethical absolute; it is only a conditional. Under some circumstances, the SPN writer might have to override the right to privacy in the interest of some other equally important moral principle, for example, the right to tell one's own story in one's own voice as honestly as possible.

Okay, I admit that ethical rules like the above are the easy part for an academic ethicist like myself to lay out.[2] But moral principles are troublesome reference points to follow with any degree of consistency precisely because, in the real world, an SPN writer can always come up with plausible exceptions to each and every one of them. The hard work, of course, is to translate these general moral principles into a flexible and usable code of ethics for SPN writers. When I first decided to write this book, for example, my ethical strategy was to treat each one of the individuals whom I mention throughout my narrative with as much care and sensitivity as possible. I asked myself these questions: In telling my own personal story, as well as my story of SPN writing, would I be able to treat all the "others" in my narrative in as respectful a way as possible, and still write honestly? If these others were to see their names and stories in print, would they feel embarrassed, ashamed, or misused? Would they cringe at my violation of their privacy?

In particular, I worried about Pamela, whom I wrote about in chapter 4. I knew from personal conversations with her that she agonized about the ethical ramifications of exposing her father as an incest predator and, in the process, indirectly implicating her mother and sisters, who were innocent characters in her incest story. Would I be compounding the ethical issues by retelling her story and reouting all the characters in her family narrative once again? Would I be double-jeopardizing them, and Pamela, so to speak? Did I have a right to do this? Did I even have a right to write this particular paragraph because of the risk of violating a confidence?

I remember Pamela asking me, during the time she was writing her dissertation, the following question: "Is what I'm doing ethically justifiable?" I could only answer in my usual postmodern fashion—it all depends. On what? you are probably asking. By way of a personal response, let me continue telling my story of writing this book. My ethical rule of thumb throughout was to be as truthful about SPN, my teaching of it, and my personal and professional experiences with students and colleagues around it, as I possibly could be.

I knew that there would be times in this book when my need to be honest would infringe on the privacy of others. I also knew that most of the time it would not. I did realize, though, that some ethical fallout was inevitable because I wanted to tell my story candidly and dramatically. I wanted to reveal my truth in an unfettered manner. In all instances, I wanted to be damned sure that I did this with respect, generosity, and fairmindedness. I didn't want my honesty to be a pretext for settling old scores or for annihilating those whom I perceived to be enemies of SPNs. Neither did I want to tell stories out of school in order to show off my insider status or to embarrass those whom I thought might be hostile. I wanted, instead, to be a conciliatory voice in schools of education, and other professional units, in arguing for the value of SPN scholarship.

I am confident that I followed my own SPN code of ethics in a responsible and consistent way. I made it a point to get all the major players I mentioned in my SPN to review what I wrote about them, even though I did not have to. I am lucky that the eight writers in the previous two chapters gave me permission to analyze my relationship with them, and to discuss their materials, in print. But what if they had refused to give me official permission? After all, their theses and dissertations were public documents on full display in at least three places around my university, including the university and the college libraries. Similarly, their defenses were public forums. Would I have published their stories anyway? It all depends.

My answer to Pamela's question went something like the following, and I know that it will sound like a moral copout to those of you who are far more certain about the rightness and wrongness of human behavior than I am. So be it. I will proceed anyway. I believe that moral purity and ethical perfection are unachievable in any type of human endeavor, but especially in trying to do truthful writing about oneself. Moral certitude is one thing. Moral discernment is another. In my opinion, SPN writers need to be morally discerning, not morally certain. Moral discernment is about making prudent distinctions. SPN writers will need to know when it's necessary, and when it's defensible, to make moral compromises in order to compose narratives that are cogent and honest. Knowing when and how to compromise is the basic challenge of living an ethical life; and, I will add, in writing powerful SPNs as well.

If Pamela had decided to keep her incest narrative a secret, she would have compromised the truth of her central construct: We need to tell our stories in all their ugliness, as well as in all their glory, if we are to face the truth in ourselves, and if we want to get others to do the same. Telling our *whole* story, without putting on blinkers, often requires an act of courage. In weighing two conflicting goods—keeping her parents', and family's, secret against risking everything to tell her own truth—Pamela decided to tell her truth. She did this, I believe, with passion, resilience, and faith.

In all candor, though, any type of writing in academia that involves others always benefits the researcher-scholar in some way. Daphne Patai zeroes in on this point with her characteristic bluntness: "The fact remains that it is *we* who are using *them* for *our* books [theses, dissertations, research projects, etc.]."[3] Thus, research and scholarship of all kinds, even in the sciences, are, at the core, self-aggrandizing and self-interested, and always in the researcher-scholar's favor. We (experts) benefit; they (subjects) risk. Whether this is right or wrong is a moot moral point. We do use *them*, period.

Furthermore, our relationships with these others will always be asymmetrical. In Marxist language, we experts exert full control over the means and ends of production. Even the notion of "informed consent" is ambiguous, because consent from "them" must always be given in the languages, and stories, that we scholars construct and impose. The trick, of course, is to acknowledge that we do, indeed, use others in our research for our own ends; but to be scrupulous in using these others in the best, ethical manner. What's best and what's ethical? Ah, here we face the question of subjective moral discernment once again.

Here's my subjective moral discernment on the question—no matter how ethically fastidious you would like to be in writing an SPN, there will always be moral compromises you need to make. Pamela understood the ethical risks in going public, and you should, too. Furthermore, like her, you will find that, after the fact, there might have been other roads you could have taken in order to achieve your ends. You will also identify statements you wish you had withheld, and personal confidences you wanted to maintain, yet didn't. But—and this is a huge qualifying "but"—I am convinced that the achievement of ethical perfection in writing SPNs comes only in hindsight. This is because I believe we live ethics mostly backward, not forward. We make the moral leap, and then we spend the aftermath agonizing over whether we did the right thing. How could it be otherwise? Do you know a single person who has never once second-guessed a moral decision? I don't.

Granted the validity of all that I've said about the inevitability of ethical imperfection in SPN writing, however, I maintain that it is still important for all of us to realize that we do not live our lives cut off from others. Our stories overlap with other stories. Telling our stories will inevitably implicate others, whether we like it or not. The ethical key, however, is to keep the following types of questions constantly in mind: Why are you disclosing another's secrets? How does a particular violation of privacy serve your narrative's purposes? Is there another way that you could have made the same point? Are you showing respect for yourself, as well as for the other, in writing about the other? Does the other deserve your respect? Have you objectified the other in any way? If so, why? Have you given the other's side of the story? What are your moral boundaries in transgressing the private life of another? Is there a point beyond which you will not go?

Would you want someone to write this type of disclosure about you? How ethically pivotal is the principle of honesty, and the right to tell your truth in your own best way, in your SPN writing? Under what conditions would you override the principle of honesty in your storytelling with the principle of protecting the privacy of those who inhabit your narrative? Or vice versa?

In the end, I remarked to Pamela, when all is said and done, the most ethical decision regarding the protection of another person's privacy in SPN writing will be based on a subjective act of moral discernment. And the decision you make will depend on your particular situation, your intentions, your own narrative background, your desired outcomes, and your purposes for writing an SPN in the first place. In other words, when the privacy rights of others are in conflict with your right to maintain your personal integrity and voice, you will have to rely on your own subjective judgment to resolve the dilemma. No outside authority, moral rubric, or ethical absolute will ever render your decision foolproof or beyond critique. The story is everything, and everyone's story is different. Like all else, moral decisions will always be bounded by the contingencies of particular stories. Once again, in Sartre's language, there is no exit. Here's my ethical advice for SPN writers then, for what it's worth: be honest, be empathic, tell your story as only you can, and then move quickly out of the range of fire.

Truth: Are Facts the Same as Truth?

Right off, let me give my unequivocal answer to the question I raise in this section heading: yes and no. Close readers will observe that I have used the word "truth" often in the section that immediately precedes this one. Am I, then, a hypocritical postmodernist? Some of you may wonder how I can use the words "truth" and "story" in the same breath, and be a scholar whose intellectual integrity is still intact. Not to worry. Give me a little while to explain. You may or may not agree with what I have to say, but at least you'll understand a little more about my own story of truth. I know that I talked about a postmodern-philosophical conception of truth in chapter 2, but I want to take a different tack here. I am mainly interested, at this point, in discussing how to reconfigure your more conventional understandings of truth when you begin writing SPNs. So please bear with me.

In talking about how the first draft of his memoir *Growing Up* was a disaster because it had no narrative tension and no credible hook, Russell Baker made a comment in print that shocked some of my students when they read it. Just before he began to write a completely new second draft of his memoir, he said: "I decided that although nobody's life makes any sense, if you're going to make a book out of it you might as well make it into a story. I remember saying to my wife, 'I am now going upstairs to invent the story of my life.'"[4] Several students wondered aloud if Baker, therefore, had given himself permission to lie in his memoir. Could he really be trusted to tell the true story of his life, if he was going to "invent" it? Was Baker saying that all personal writing is fiction? If so, then what was the "truth" he was trying to tell in his story, and how could he tell it truthfully?

In my opinion, many of these students were mistakingly equating *facts* with *truth*; as well as confusing truth telling with storytelling. I think it important to distinguish two notions of truth in writing SPNs, in addition to *philosophical* truth, which I discussed in chapter 2. I call these "ethical truth" and "narrative truth." *Ethical truth* is being truthful: honest, veracious, not lying, not deliberately intending to deceive; trying to render as accurate an account of the facts as you understand them. Thus, a truthful SPN writer is someone who is not deliberately trying to mislead or deceive the reader. Truthfulness in SPN writing is being as honest as possible about what one remembers, feels, knows, and senses about events and people, both from the past and in the present. This is ethical truth, and it has everything to do with an author's motives, intentions, and attempts to be accurate.

My educated hunch is that readers discover very, very quickly when an SPN writer is not being ethically truthful. An author's dishonesty sooner or later calls attention to itself. We just know when the writer is over the top with hyperbole or deliberately distorting content and facts in the story. We sense when the author is being insincere and disingenuous. How do we know this? Aside from a strong intuitive feeling that something has gone awry in the text, we know that the facts in the narrative just don't add up. They are inconsistent and contradictory. The account is full of inaccuracies, or else the story is so blatantly loaded against, or for, something or somebody, that we know it is false.

Then our mistrust alarms begin to sound, softly at first, and then loudly, until eventually they blare. When your mistrust alarms go off, I believe this is a pretty good indication that the author is not telling the ethical truth. My advice to you is to close the book and move on. Or if you yourself are tempted to be untruthful in your SPN, stop writing and ask yourself this question: What exactly is my motivation in distorting the facts as I know them? And remember, distortion is different from interpretation. The former is calculated to deceive, the latter is inevitable, because no fact ever comes to us as an immaculate perception.

You need to ask yourself this question when tempted to distort: Could I justify this distortion in front of a jury of my peers, or in front of the person being distorted? If your answer is no, then I recommend that you delete your content and start over. I can truthfully (notice my adverb) say that the eight narrativists in the two previous chapters did not lie to me or to their committees. Their facts corresponded to other facts in their narratives. They avoided distortion. There was internal coherence in their respective narratives. I trusted them intuitively and intellectually. They were telling the ethical truth. No bells sounded.

But then there is the author who has let the privilege of literary license run amok. For this type of author, the lie is justified because it makes the narrative more dramatic, the issues more black and white, the characters more "real" and polarized. Certain kinds of literary license are allowable in SPN writing in order to sustain narrative interest and maintain artistic economy. For example, facts can be rearranged chronologically. Scenes and characters can be composited. Time can be compressed, and some details can be left out. Also, SPN writers can use disclaimers such as "I imagine," or "to the best of my recollection." But SPN writers can overuse, and overextend, all of these conventions.

Literary license has a habit of sneaking out of control. A little license here, a little there, and before you know it, you've contaminated the whole manuscript with half-truths and lies. The truth center of the narrative disappears. The whole thing reeks. Although it hasn't happened yet, I know what I would do if I felt that one of my SPN graduate students was deliberately falsifying data in order to advance a lopsided agenda of one kind or another. How would I know this? My mistrust alarm would sound. I would start to ask questions, tough ones. I would grow uneasy with untruthful answers. Even though the student might vehemently disagree with my assessment, I would threaten to remove myself from the committee. I would insist that unless the thesis or dissertation underwent a thorough revision, with all the distortions and falsifications completely removed, I would be out of the picture.

Narrative truth, however, is something quite different from ethical truth, although there are points of intersection. Where these points lie depends on an author's ethical discernment. Let me tell you a little story. This episode took place when I first started my doctoral work at Boston

University in 1965. It was the day that I was scheduled to meet my as-signed doctoral advisor for the first time, the person who many experts in the field considered to be the premier philosopher of education in the world, Theodore Brameld. I, the graduate of a mediocre state college, was very nervous about meeting this August eminence. I stammered continually during the interview whenever he questioned me about my academic and blue-collar background.

Here is what I vividly remember about Brameld: the shock of snow-white hair, the glasses pulled down to the tip of his nose, the way he peered at me over those glasses, the fact that he was much better dressed than I, and, most of all, his bemused tone of voice and attitude as he listened to me make an absolute fool of myself. I sensed from his ques-tions that he wasn't there to cut me down to size. He really wanted to know me better as a person. Was I someone with whom he could work effectively during the course of my doctoral studies? But I still felt I needed to sell myself. And so I babbled self-serving nonsense for what seemed like hours.

Finally, when I finished with my pathetic explanation of who I was, and what my goals for the doctoral program were, Brameld said: "You don't need to impress me or brownnose me. You were accepted into this program because we felt you had unlimited intellectual potential. We still do. I'm as pleased to have you as my doctoral student as you claim you are to have me as your academic advisor. So loosen up, stop summa-rizing your resume, and let's talk about why you love philosophy so much." And I did.

I think he was impressed. I remember leaving Brameld's office fly-ing so high that I didn't touch down until I reached home. That evening my wife heard more about my interview than she probably wanted to, after her long, difficult day teaching in an urban elementary school class-room. I wouldn't be where I am today without that man's enormous influence on my life. The theme of this little story is that often our men-tors choose us rather than the other way around. I was just too intimi-dated at our first meeting to think of Brameld's ever being my philo-sophical guide and professorial sponsor. I thought I sounded so much like an unmitigated jerk that he would want nothing to do with me. But, over time, he became both my mentor and friend. I am forever grateful for his example and his support. He recognized, and affirmed, some-thing in me that I couldn't see in myself.

Actually, I wrote about this same meeting in my intellectual mem-oir, which I mentioned earlier: *Spirituality, Ethics, Religion, and Teaching: A Professor's Journey.*[5] When I match that account with this one, there are many similarities, but some of the details, and general impressions, differ. In the earlier book, I didn't include as many specifics about the meeting as I did here. I didn't mention my stammering. I painted a somewhat different picture in my book of my future advisor as someone who didn't talk much to me; he only listened. He didn't put me quite as much at ease as I mention here. His questions were few and far between. And while the overall tone of his comments was the same, some of the content of the interview was different from what I narrate here in this book.

Taking a longer view, however, I wonder if my present-day account of an event that took place almost 40 years ago was factually based. Did I get it right? Was this man's hair really that white? Did he wear his glasses down near the tip of his nose? Did he even have his reading glasses on? Was he actually dressed better than I? Did he use the term "brownnose?" Did I tell and retell the story of this interview to my wife when she came home? I can attest to the accuracy of what lawyers call "provable facts": I met this man in his office at Boston University in the fall of 1965. He was world-renowned. I know that I was full of anxiety, because I was always nervous in new situations that I thought might be threatening. And I know that upon leaving his office, I felt better about being assigned to him as an advisee. After all, I didn't switch advisors during the next three years.

But I can't say for sure that everything else happened that day in 1965 in exactly the way I describe it here. Does this mean that I am a liar? Did I deliberately fudge or hyperbolize the facts? Am I playing games with the truth? No—in my mind, every sentence I wrote above represents the truth as I perceive it today. I am not a liar. I am not trying deliberately to deceive anyone, including myself. What is happening here is that my narrative truth informs, and re-forms, my ethical truth, as it does for every SPN writer I know. What do I mean by this?

Here's what I'm getting at. The SPN writer's story is always selective. In Virginia Woolf's language, "Fact is not necessarily the same as truth."[6] I may have gotten some of the details wrong about my meeting with my eminent professor in 1965 because everyone's detail-based memory fades over time. But more important, in Woolf's sense, I cannot escape the universal fate of all SPN writers: as we try to recall our pasts, we inevitably reconstruct them.

The past is never indelibly fixed in our memories. It is always changing, according to our present situations, moods, and perspectives. We remember *then* according to what we need, feel, and think *now*. We may never be able to change what occurred in the past, but we can change how we view the past. If I had written about my encounter with Theodore Brameld one week, or one year, or one decade later than when it first happened, I am certain that my narrative would have depended on who I was at the time I was writing about it.

This is narrative truth, and it differs distinctly from ethical truth. As I try to recall specific events from almost 40 years ago in my writer's mind, I am actually re-creating my past. I am informing and re-forming it. This is what Russell Baker meant when he said that he was about to "invent" his life. He was about to live his life twice, once in the past and once in the present. And he knew that his present life would alter his past life both spiritually and historically.

For several years after I finished my doctorate degree, I tried to distance myself from my advisor's influence, because I wanted to make my own way in the academic world, out from under the impress of his large shadow. As some Zen Buddhists might say, I was in the process of "killing" my Buddha so that I might become the Buddha myself. But, from the perspective of almost four decades later, as I write this book, I have no need at all to kill my Buddha.[7] In fact, I want to venerate my advisor's memory. And what I've said in the last several paragraphs is the total narrative truth, so help me, Virgina Woolf. Moreover, in my opinion as an obviously self-interested writer, it's the ethical truth as well. *Total* ethical truth? Probably not. Well-intended? Incontrovertibly.

Okay, here is my almost-final word on narrative truth. Truth, in my opinion, is what happens when you decide to write for the reasons that Nancy Slonim Aronie writes:

> We write to tell the truth. We write to know who we are. We write to find our voices. We write to save the world. We write to save ourselves. We write so that when we look back and see that moment when we were totally clear, completely brilliant, and astoundingly wise, there is proof—proof right there on the goddamn page. And we can read our words and say, "I wrote that." And if we did it once—we can do it again.[8]

Politics:
Why Do Certain Discourses Get Privileged in the Academy?

I want to begin this section with three separate stories about politics and SPNs. I will circle back to each of them later in order to respond to the question I ask in the heading of this section. These stories represent, to the best of my narrative recollection, what actually happened during the past few years. All the characters are real, and the setting was always the same—my favorite restaurant hangout, Chef's Corner, in Williston, Vermont.

Three Stories

Let me call my first story "The Public Intellectual." During a leisurely breakfast, a young, untenured faculty member and I talked for almost two hours, over an open-egg sandwich and a bowl of granola. I look forward to being with this woman, not only because I sense that she likes my company, but also because I thoroughly enjoy her vitality. She has an infectious zest for living a personal life that is authentic and joyful. She evinces a professional commitment to her work as a teacher-educator that is inspiring. And she possesses a profound spiritual conviction that, in the end, life is sacred, people are wonderful, and love is the necessary condition for all of us to come together in order to experience those fleeting signals of immanence and transcendence that give our lives meaning.

But she can also be a pragmatist and a bit of a worrier. She's struggling, two years into her time on a tenure-track position, with this all-too-common issue: Can she achieve tenure as much on her own terms as on the academy's terms? She's a wife, mother, intellectual, teacher, writer, colleague, and dear friend to many. While trained as a social scientist, she also sees herself as a public intellectual. She enjoys doing the kind of writing that I am talking about in these chapters—personal narrative writing that attempts to bridge the gaping chasm that often separates the academy from the public schools, and writing that tries to communicate her wisdom to her family and friends in a jargon-free style so that they might be able to understand and appreciate her ideas. She wants desperately to be a border crosser, and yet, like all young faculty members, she still needs some assurance that the academy values her work in such a way that she will eventually earn tenure and promotion.

I tell the public intellectual that there are no guarantees and, of course, she knows this. She has already been told by higher-ups in her department that in order to get tenure she must publish in refereed, scholarly journals and write books for prestigious university presses. An article in a so-called non–scholarly magazine with a readership of almost a million people will not do. Neither will a monograph count as serious scholarship that is published by a professional association reaching tens of thousands of readers. Why not? Because this association does not send out manuscripts to external academic reviewers. It keeps all submitted manuscripts in-house for internal review. I know from firsthand experience that these internal reviews are much tougher than the more conventional ones.

The public intellectual is growing concerned, and a little bit fatalistic. There is no question that she can do what the university sees as acceptable scholarship. I have read her dissertation, and it is brilliant. It wouldn't take much for her to shape it up for publication, as so many young, and older, faculty members do, in order to enlarge the research sections of their résumés.

The best that we can ever do in the academy, I say to her from the privileged perch of someone who is a tenured full professor, is to tell our stories, in our own words, and let the rewards fall where they may. Somewhere, I am convinced, there is a faculty evaluation committee, a department chair, and a dean who will find the wisdom in her stories to be tenurable. The public intellectual nods politely and sighs, and I think that deep down she would like to believe this. But she still looks very worried. I don't blame her. In the eyes of too many professors who sit on faculty evaluation committees, writing for a lay public is seen as a debasement of genuine scholarship.

Let me call my second story "The Novelist." Sometimes my students refer to my favorite breakfast restaurant, Chef's Corner, as "Robert's Corner," because I'm there so much. Behind my back, though, I've been told that some call it "No-bullshit Corner," because over a leisurely, two-hour breakfast, small talk gets used up very quickly. It doesn't take long to get to the meta-agenda; or what one of my students refers to as the "elephant sitting in the back corner of the restaurant that everyone knows is in the room, but nobody wants to talk about in the first few minutes."

The novelist, a doctoral student, e-mailed me one day and asked to get together. I was surprised. She had been a student in one of my earlier SPN courses. She appeared to be diligent, but she didn't say much during the term, and she made no effort to get to know me outside of class. I do recall that in one class she got very upset over the direction the conversation was going. She said something like this to the rest of us: "Why does everyone here think that SPN writing is so unorthodox and threatening to the academy? Just find allies, stop whining, and start writing." Someone asked her if she was thinking of doing an SPN dissertation, and she answered without hesitation, "Hell, no. I'm doing a qualitative study, and I'm almost finished collecting my data. I might try to find a way to work some SPN stuff into my writing, though. Maybe I'll end up doing a hybrid type of study. Don't worry. It's my dissertation, and *I'll* tell my advisor, and my committee, how I want to do it. *They* won't tell me."

This was two years earlier. But now, during her breakfast with me, she confronts her "elephant" very quickly: "Robert, would you be willing to advise my dissertation if I were to write a novel?" Gulp! "I thought you were wrapping up a qualitative dissertation," I replied. "No, I got bogged down during the year after I took your course, but this had nothing to do with your course. I just couldn't follow through, because I lost interest in my topic. A lot of serious, personal setbacks have happened in my life since then. I felt that I let down a lot of people in dropping out of the doctoral picture, including myself. Now, I think my advisor has lost faith in me, and this hurts. I don't know where to turn."

"A novel? Why a novel?" I ask. She responds, "Because, as an English major in college, I took a lot of creative writing courses. I've actually been working on a novel for the last two years, and I'm one chapter away from finishing it. I can't think of a project that's been more relevant to everything that's been going on in my life, both personally and professionally. I've poured my life into this writing. If I can brag a little, I think I've got something really innovative and useful for educators here. I just need you to read it, tell me what needs to be done with it, and I'll work my butt off to shape it up so that it will be something both you and I can be proud of. What do you think?"

What did I think? What did Robert, the outlier, think? What did Robert, the interdisciplinary border crosser, think? What did Robert, the academic subversive, think? What did Robert, the humanist, think? What did Robert, the ally, think? Listen to what I said to the novelist: "Jeez, this isn't a department of English, you know. This is a professional school. I wouldn't even know how to evaluate the scholarly dimension of a novel.

"Don't get me wrong. I like your willingness to transgress the narrow boundaries of what we faculty think is professional research, but this idea takes us into totally unchartered territory. Couldn't you find a way to make your novel an SPN? I don't even know who we could get to sit on your committee. Let's rethink this, and meet once more." As she gets up to leave, I breathe a sigh of relief. Maybe, after she thinks about it some more, she'll abandon the idea of writing a novel for her dissertation. Maybe she'll come to her senses.

I never saw her, or heard from her again. Today, in looking back at that meeting with the novelist, I am embarrassed. At that moment, Robert's "no-bullshit corner" became "come to Robert's Corner, and watch him do a bullshit dance like nobody else can." The novelist had called my bluff. I found myself fearing for my reputation when she mentioned the word "novel." How would I ever sell the idea of a novel to my colleagues? Would this set back my initiative to get faculty recognition for SPN dissertations? Shouldn't I be worried about my, and the college's, intellectual credibility? What the hell did I know about writing a novel? I'd be the laughingstock of my professional college, and the college would be the laughingstock of the university. How could I be an ally to this? No way, baby.

Let me call my third story "The Moral Activist." This is how the moral activist describes himself: "I am Chicano, which is a bountiful blend of indigenous, Mexican, and American identities." I choose to call this man a *moral* activist because, while he is certainly concerned with changing the university system politically, he chooses to do this on his *own* terms, rather than on the terms of any specific political movement. He wants to do this in a mutually respectful way, in a conversation that starts with where people are rather than where he wants them to be. Unfortunately, "activism" is a word that has been expropriated by extremist political movements of all types. Historically, and etymologically (L, *agere*), though, "activism" connotes something very different from the extremist stereotype: It means taking "positive" steps to achieve a worthy end. The moral activist is keenly aware of this truer meaning of activism.

He wants all of his interventions to be compassionate and generous, as well as passionate and full of conviction. He wants to work hand in hand with people of all ethnicities and races, both within and without the academy, in order to enhance everyone's humanity. For us to reduce him to a "political" identity only would be to narrow all of his work in the academy to a political stereotype: the angry Chicano militant. This restrictive political narrative just doesn't work for him. There are many more dimensions to the moral activist than the political, although the latter descriptor is certainly important in understanding the intensity of his overall mission.

The moral activist is one of the nicest human beings I have ever met. He is my friend and advisee. He is an extraordinary listener, a gifted questioner, and a superbly intuitive reader of human beings and what makes them tick. He came into my life five years ago and, after graduating with his master's degree, he went on for his doctorate in higher education administration. Our relationship is close. Sometimes I get the impression that I push him too much, although he has never told me this. I consider him like a son. I don't know what he would think of this designation, though.

During the time I have known him, the moral activist has been very conscious of his ethnicity. He talks of the obstacles he has overcome in order to succeed in white America. While a student in my courses, he would tell his personal stories every so often in papers and in classroom conversations. He is a brilliant and sensitive storyteller, and so he gets, and keeps, people's attention. He is very proud of his working-class background: a first-generation community college student, a West Coast fisherman, later, a graduate of a four-year university, a graduate of one of the best master's degree programs in higher education administration in the country, a winner of a prestigious fellowship from the Gates Millennium Foundation, and now, someone working on his doctoral dissertation. But I was not aware, in his own language, of "the rage that dwells within me." He conceals it well beneath a pleasant exterior.

Over breakfast, one of many meals he and I have shared together in the past several years, the moral activist is reflective. "I want to do an SPN for my dissertation, Robert, but I'm up in the air about it." "Why?" I ask. "I've never talked with you about this before, but I feel as if I am living a dual existence. I am both inside and outside the academy. To my family and friends in my old neighborhood, I am a highly educated person who has bettered himself beyond belief. To the university community, despite all the wonderful people I've met who have supported me over the years, I am still the outsider, the infamous 'other.' Who the hell am I, then? What I want is to be free . . . free of my own mental shackles that bind and constrict the very sense of who I am. I am many selves."

"Why are you having so much trouble deciding on whether to do an SPN for your dissertation?" I ask. "Robert, I'll be honest. Will an SPN dissertation be respected in the academy? Will it be respected by folks in my Chicano community? Why do some faculty whom I value here raise their eyebrows, roll their eyes, and frown, all ever so slightly, whenever I mention that I might write an SPN? Will my family and friends think that an SPN is the easy way out because it doesn't look or sound anything like what they've heard a traditional dissertation should be? I feel so damned schizophrenic. I know that I have a right to do a dissertation in my own voice on my own terms, and I want to. But I also have a need to make good on the academy's terms. I want respect. I don't want any favors. I doubt that I would be punishing myself this way if I were white. I'm pissed off—at the racism in American culture, and in the university, for creating the seeds of self-doubt within me. But I'm also angry at the conventional scholarly culture of the university for making me feel that I've got to make a choice."

Politics

Politics: "That which affects, or acts according to, the interests of status and authority in an organization" Oxford English Dictionary. The principle that all human behavior is political has become a cliché, especially in the academy. "The personal is the political, and the political is the personal" was the mantra of 1960s and 1970s feminism. I am interested, however, in talking about politics as that which has to do with the practice of holding onto influence, status, and authority in the university. This is a notion of politics that graduate students, and new faculty members, find daunting upon first encounter. How many times have I heard these folks say in their own way: "This place is really political. I had no idea that politics was so important in the community of scholars. Shouldn't we be above all this?"

No, we shouldn't. No, we can't. I don't necessarily think of university politics as being ipso facto evil. There are times, I would argue, when I might have a moral responsibility to be political. I might have to hold onto, even wield, my power in order to bring about a greater good for students and colleagues. For example, I am always politicking, calling in my chits so to speak, in order to increase the writing options for those students who want to do SPN manuscripts. I am ever on the prowl for faculty allies to serve on SPN thesis and dissertation committees. I do them favors; they do me favors. I am a political animal. There is no survival in the academy unless one has mastered the art and practice of politics. Love the university; love its politics. There is no other way.

For me, politics becomes corrupt, however, when it serves the interests *only* of the powerful to the complete exclusion of the powerless; and whenever it renders those without power even more powerless than they were to begin with. Politics, in brief, is a means to an end. If politics morphs into an end in itself, as it often does in the university, then the chances are that it is nothing more than a prop for the interests of those in power, and this includes academic disciplines, unions, trustees, top-tier administrators, chairs, directors, and professors.

The *public intellectual* I described earlier in this section needs to understand that the kind of scholarship she would like to do threatens the research status quo of her professional unit. Thus, it calls into question the unit's power to insist that all of its faculty, without exception, master and produce certain types of research and scholarship in order to attain reappointment, promotion, and tenure. Mastery and production of the conventional means of research and scholarship are the nontenured faculty's tickets for admission to the club. These tickets also assure continuity of the time-tested research and scholarly conventions. A term that critical theorists use to describe an authority's completely dominating influence is "hegemony." Although the term itself is ugly, its meaning is appropriate for who determines what counts as acceptable research in the academy.

On the other hand, SPN writing by professors, either in or out of the academy, but particularly in professional schools, is considered to be marginalized writing. This is because the gatekeepers of academic norms think of SPN writing as synonymous with what public intellectuals do. I am speaking here of journalists, media pundits, or online writers. Check out the more autobiographical work of such star public intellectuals as Marian Wright Edelman, Anne Lamott, Annie Dillard, William F. Buckley, Andrew Sullivan, James Carroll, and Richard Rodriguez. I'd be willing to bet that, in my college, for example, very few colleagues have ever required the works of these authors in their courses.

One of the major, latent functions of university research and scholarship is to limit the faculty member's reach primarily to members of a respective discipline. This function serves the purpose of encouraging the important internal conversations that ultimately deepen and refine the ideas in an academic or professional discipline. It also enhances and solidifies the authority of the gatekeepers of the discipline to decide what goes and what doesn't, who comes and who leaves. This isn't all bad, but neither is it all good. We have seen too often how people of color, women, and assorted intellectual heretics get forced out of the university because they are bold enough to challenge the hegemony of the older research-scholarship models.

But my colleague, the public intellectual, wants to be more expansive and more democratic. She wants to reach out to those folks who don't inhabit the university space; who don't speak her professional discipline's highly technical language; who don't care about the complex, finer points of her discipline that are as much about maintaining political power and scoring academic points as they are about anything substantive. She wants to publish her material in the largest newspaper in the state. She seeks writing outlets in mass-market journals and magazines. She might even consider an electronic publication, if this medium will extend her access to more of the lay public.

My advice to my public intellectual colleague might seem like the compromise position of someone thoroughly socialized by the academy, and it probably is. But I'll give it anyway. Try to be both a guerilla public intellectual *and* a university scholar. Don't get sucked into either-or thinking. There is no reason why you can't present your work in two dialects: university-speak and lay-speak. Do the research and scholarship that you need to do in order to benefit from the university's conventional reward system. Do the public communication you want to do in order to find your true satisfaction.

By the way, you will not need to do as much conventional research and scholarship as you think. Nowadays, faculty reward and assessment committees, even at Research 1 Carnegie institutions, look at the full range of professorial activity and achievement. I know; I have served on a number of faculty evaluation committees over the years. I have seen successful grantsmen and grantswomen get tenure and promotion. I have seen minimal publishers and outstanding teachers and service providers get tenure and promotion. I have seen politically astute, university citizens receive tenure and promotion. It's just too easy, I have noticed over the years, to scare yourself, imagine the worst, surrender to your fears, and shut down. The mystique of the Terrible Tenure Track Trauma is greater than its reality.

If you want to stop doing conventional scholarly research after you receive tenure, then this is your call. I know many of your colleagues who have done exactly this, and they still get up in the morning and manage to live a good life. But you could also seriously consider doing the writing of the public intellectual along with the writing of the university scholar, both before *and* after receiving tenure. I also know several colleagues who have made this call, including myself. We, too, live a good and happy life.

And, so, here is my recommendation in a nutshell, my public intellectual friend: go ahead and translate your more academic work into an accessible idiom for laypersons, educated or otherwise. This dual type of writing is very achievable, and could even make you some money, if this is your goal. Parker Palmer, Cornell West, Gary Wills, bell hooks, Henry Louis Gates, Diana Eck, Carol Gilligan, Nikki Giovanni, Edward Said, and Sara Lawrence-Lightfoot, among many others, are academic luminaries who have done a series of memoirs, autobiographies, op ed pieces, and other forms of personal writing that have been well received by the lay public.

I think it revealing that at majestic Harvard University, Lawrence Buell, chair of the English department, is in the process of building a department filled with public intellectuals. In the last year alone, he has hired Louis Menand, a literary critic and historian; and James Wood, a writer for *The New Republic*. He has also recruited the novelists Jamaica Kincaid, Azdie Smith, and Amitav Ghosh to teach in the department. Only Menand has a doctorate. Here is what Buell has said about his hiring practices:

> I want to blur the borders between the academy and the nonacademy. . . . We're not going to be fussy about the fact that [these hires] are not coming from an academic background. Value is value. . . . Border-

crossing, whether between disciplines or crossing outside the academic tribe, is not only valuable for our students, it keeps the rest of us invigorated.[9]

All the above scholars, by the way, have also been well remunerated; as well as being the beneficiaries of tenure and promotion, grants and awards, honorary degrees and distinguished chairs, at their respective academic institutions. But you don't need to aim as high to get your way. You do need to aim for something, though, if you are to give all of your audiences a chance to recognize, and reward, your talents. Build your reputation; secure your authority and influence at the university by being both an academic *and* a public intellectual. At the very least, your dual set of accomplishments will keep your more envious colleagues guessing as to what successes will come next for you. This is fun, believe me.

I may have blown it earlier with the *novelist*, but I'm back to try to redeem myself. I hope that she is reading this. If she were to have breakfast with me now, here is what I would say to her: "So you want to do a novel, hey? Tell me why, so I can better understand how both of us can make this happen in a professional school." And then I would listen to her novelist's narrative, being especially attentive to any overlap that might exist between her narrative and my SPN narrative. If I couldn't find any intersection, I would back off and meet her fully on her own terms. But I would also see it as my responsibility to educate her about the politics of dissertation advising, and the purpose of dissertation writing, in a research university, and in a professional school.

Here's another take on the politics of scholarship: certain types of writing get privileged over others in the university because the conventions and traditions of the disciplines dictate what's acceptable and what isn't. Critical theorists would say that the privileging of certain discourses guarantees the superiority of one scholarly genre over another, thereby reinforcing, and perpetuating, the status of particular research methodologies. Although I'm not very comfortable with the critical-theory slant of the language in this definition of politics (this type of nomenclature is fast becoming a cliché in cultural studies programs, and so it is losing its pop!), it does make a significant point. Anytime that you want to do something different by way of scholarship or research in the university, whether it requires a drastic or moderate change, you are talking about shaking up established hierarchies of intellectual authority.

Thus, you will need to be attentive to the rites of initiation into the disciplines that lead to scholarly conformity everywhere in the academy. You will need first to be an initiate before you can become an innovator.

Such has the academy been, such is it now, and such will it be. Although this may sound depressingly deterministic, I also believe that the academy is porous in its interstices. There are soft spots everywhere, and you can poke and prod them in some very effective ways. But first you need to find them.

As I suggested in an analysis of my overcautious response to the novelist when I first talked with her during breakfast, I too am a member of the university's intellectual hierarchy. I might be playing around with change at the periphery of the system, but I still represent what the institution values by way of acceptable research and scholarship. Nevertheless, I have spent the last several years looking for the soft spots in the research-scholarship system of my college. One of the ways to learn where the soft spots are is to learn the certified academic language. Read the scholarly journals. Listen to the jargon consistently being tossed about at conferences. Learn to speak the language well. Then you will be able to stretch its meanings, and make it fit your own purposes.

Think of your discipline's approved approach to formal academic writing as nothing more than a story about what's in and what's out in the field. And then reframe the story ever so gently at first, more radically as time goes on. Be aware always, however, that you are a heartbeat away from becoming a fierce defender, and protector, of your own reframed research-scholarship paradigm, if you manage to alter the conventional system in any way. It will happen gradually, imperceptibly, but it will happen.

And before long, insurgent intellectuals will be challenging the exclusivity of *your* paradigm; gently at first, more radically as time goes on. This could even be the fate of SPNs in my professional school. Twenty years from now, I might even be hearing talk of SPN hegemony. I actually had a nightmare about this recently: lots of young, second-generation critical pedagogues like Henry Giroux running around, claiming that SPNs are nothing more than counterrevolutionary tools of the elitist-oppressor class.

I'll never forget the comment of one of my colleagues in the English department who brought me up short one day. A professor of writing, he was a member of a thesis committee for one of my students who was defending an SPN. At the end of the student's defense, my colleague made the following comment: "I liked your thesis very much, but why did you have to muck it up with scholarly citations, universalizable themes, and references to readings. Why didn't you just tell your story in your good creative way, let your readers figure out all its meanings, and let it go at that? Show, don't tell." In one well-intended comment, my colleague unwittingly blew apart my "ten tentative SPN guidelines."

In my colleague's creative writing department, personal narrative can stand on its own as an intellectual activity. A whole different set of criteria legitimizes personal narrative writing as appropriate scholarship. This type of writing doesn't need what he considered to be the embroidery of conceptual analysis, authorial citations, and footnoting. In my school, however, personal narrative writing needs the backup of scholarly research if it is to count as "valid research." It's got to resemble conventional scholarship if it is to be marketable at the university.

Each department and school has its peculiar initiation and maintenance rites. Each has its scholarly presuppositions. Each operates out of a prior narrative as to what counts as scholarship and what doesn't. Each knows intuitively what a "good" piece of academic writing looks like, smells like, feels like, and tastes like. What I thought was scholarly, and what my colleague from the English department thought, differed markedly, even though we both deeply appreciate personal narrative writing.

What's the moral of this story? Again, let me speak directly to my novelist. You can sell your idea of doing a novel for your dissertation as long as you understand what is at risk for all the stakeholders in the process. Know that most of the stakeholders mean well. They believe passionately in the worth of the scholarly conventions of their disciplines. These conventions have proven over time to be serviceable and worthwhile. Some of them have stood the test of time because they deserved to. Some, in my opinion, should have been allowed to wither and die a long time ago. The challenge is to sort out what is still useful and what isn't. This can only be done in an atmosphere of mutual respect and sensitivity to the interests of all the involved parties. And it can only be done cooperatively and consensually. Lone wolves need not apply here.

From a political standpoint, then, you will need to learn how to be an innovator who makes allies, rather than a resister who makes enemies. Politics is an interpersonal art, not a martial art. For example, if you believe that your dissertation genre, the novel, deals in its own unique way with ideas important to the education profession, then I would argue that you have an intellectual responsibility to open up new spaces for academic discourse in your department of education. But I would also argue that you have a diplomatic responsibility to do this in such a way that both you and your stakeholders end up working with, rather than against, one another.

This entails an understanding that all the stakeholders, including yourself as the novelist, have something to gain and something to lose in the process. Also, everyone has to agree on which risks are acceptable and which aren't. Everyone needs to commit to the search for some kind of practical, and philosophical, overlap among the contesting points of view. If you are ever to succeed in gaining a genuine respect for scholarly diversity in professional schools, then the search for common ground must be ongoing and never-ending. Before you can arrive at the point of getting what you want, you also need to find a way to help others get what they want.

Is all of this advice idealistic? Of course. Is this advice proffered out of the narrative of someone who himself is a beneficiary of the scholarly status quo? Of course. Is my advice more likely to conserve the system rather than transform it? Yes, but "conserve" is too loaded a term. How about replacing it with "softening up" the system for strategic change? Is this advice something that I myself have followed in all my interactions with my own colleagues? Of course not. Does this, therefore, make me a hypocrite? No, only a flawed, but well-meaning human being, still learning how to be a good colleague.

So, I say to you, my dear novelist, I am here to support you. By all means, dissertate in your own best way, but work hard to bring others along with you. Here's a little adage for you: She who dissertates alone is less likely to succeed than she who is willing to dissertate with the support of others. Yeah, I know, it's corny, but this pretty well sums up everything that I have to say to you about the politics of writing in new formats in the university. Someday, maybe, I'll be able to offer you something more. But for now, this will have to do.

The *moral activist* is full of passion for his mission. He wants to break out of the prison of scholarly conformity. He doesn't want the academy to tell him who he is, who he ought to be, and how he ought to be a scholar. He wants to do a dissertation that talks openly about his family, his schooling, his race and Chicano identity, his language, his biculturalism, and his internalized self-hate. He hopes that through the honest telling of his complex, troubled, multilayered story, he can "disrupt the dominant narrative" of the university culture, both for his own sake and for the sake of others who are marginalized in the academy.

He knows that he can only speak for himself, and not for any generalized group of "others." But he nevertheless wants the opportunity to write himself as a Chicano educator and a moral activist. He wants his professional school, and the university at large, to support his SPN writing and research. He was taken aback recently when a top-level academic administrator, upon hearing what he was doing for a dissertation, called his work "soft." Rather than shrink in shame, the moral activist engaged this administrator in strenuous dialogue. Although the administrator was still unconvinced of the "rigor" of the moral activist's dissertation, he was far more aware of what SPN writing is really about. At the end, the moral activist entered the results of the conversation into his victory column. He had captured the academic gatekeeper's attention for a while, and gave him an earful.

I offer you yet another take on politics as it applies to underrepresented scholars in the academy. The principle of pluralism is okay as long as it advances an approved set of particular multicultural goods. Pluralism is dangerous, though, whenever it is used to challenge the dominant research-scholarship models of the university, especially those that exist in professional schools. Diversity of race, sexual orientation, gender, ethnicity, and so on is good. Diversity of scholarly approaches; interdisciplinary research; disciplinary border crossing; and multiple, creative uses of the I voice, and so on, is bad. Unless an underrepresented scholar in the humanities follows the impersonal pattern of formal intellectual discourse in writing—cite, quote, analyze, conclude, and list—then the scholarship is considered "soft." Unless empirical academic discourse in the sciences and social sciences follows the value-neutral pattern of literature review, interview, measure, experiment, analyze, conclude, and list, then the research is also labeled as "soft."

I chuckle nowadays whenever I hear scholars at my university use words like "soft" and "hard" to malign more personal forms of writing and celebrate more impersonal forms. What comes to mind is how graphically sexual these terms are, which probably explains why I hear these words used mainly by men. To put it bluntly, "soft" scholarship is scholarship without an erection. It is flaccid and powerless. It has no thrust. "Hard" scholarship is scholarship with a strong erection. It is tumescent and powerful. It stands at attention. Soft scholarship is weak and feminine. Hard scholarship is muscular and masculine. Soft scholarship droops. Hard scholarship moves upward.

These sexual connotations are rarely talked about in the university, but they are all too easy for skeptics like myself to ferret out. While they might sound offensive at first blush, I'm happy to do this, nonetheless. And I will continue to. The humanities are for the softies, particularly in professional schools; the social sciences and the sciences are for the hardies. While I do chuckle a bit at the blatantly sexual overtones of the two descriptors, I still grow angry. I wonder how students of color, and women, who want to write more personally, respond to these judgmental terms. Do some of them hear the same old, same old sexist prejudices now cloaked in the "soft-hard" language of the good-old boy intelligentsia? Is this adding insult to their injury?

The moral activist asks this question: "Shouldn't academic discourse reflect my identity?" If he believes that he is a Chicano lost in an Anglo world, shouldn't he be able to write about this? If he believes that he is a "bountiful blend of indigenous Mexican and American identities," shouldn't he be able to write about this? If he believes that he is unhappily becoming bicultural and living his life as a contradiction, shouldn't he be able to write about this? If he is looking for ways to "be in tune with [his] multiple selves," shouldn't he be able to write about this? I offer all of us academicians in higher education this mantra to chant together three times a day: *The discourse should reflect people's experience. The discourse should reflect people's experience. The discourse should reflect people's experience.*[10] Sometimes underrepresented people choose to reflect on their experience qualitatively; sometimes quantitatively; sometimes literarily; sometimes personally; and sometimes in *all,* or in *some,* of these ways at once.

Julia Alvarez is a moral and political activist, a Dominican Latina. In a wonderful essay called "On Finding a Latino Voice," she has some sage advice to offer the moral activist. I am not presumptuous enough to think I am qualified to advise him on racial matters. But I can try to distill Alvarez's wisdom into several choice bits of advice that might speak directly to him:

- Find a "comunidad" in the university that "affirms your values and customs." But realize that all "communidads" in American universities are temporary enclaves at best.
- Work on developing your own political identity first, before you "bear witness to [others'] exploitation."
- Don't try to go back. "Don't you see, you're here to stay?"
- Be aware that writing can sometimes "bridge [your] two worlds." You can overcome your "radical self-doubt" by reading about the "bicultural, bilingual" experiences of others like you, others from all races and ethnicities. And then you can write across your two worlds.
- Recognize that "we need *una literatura* [a literature] that testifies to our lives, provides acknowledgment of who we are; an exiled people, a migrant people, *mujeres en la lucha* [women in the struggle]." Write that literature in your own voice, with or without the academy's blessing. Use the fact that you straddle two worlds in your favor. Be a border crosser; an interdisciplinary, hybrid scholar, if this is your wont, and do it with your head held high. And don't accept for an instant that your work is soft. May your voice be soft, when it is necessary, but let your passion be hard. The academy will give in. It always does.
- Resist being "caged" by definitions of who you are by whites and by other people of color. Perhaps the best way to define yourself

is "through the stories and poems that do not limit [you] to a simple label."

- Don't target your writing only to people of Latino origin, though. "Feed the sea, feed the sea. The little rivers dry up in the long run, but the sea grows. What matters is the great body of all that has been thought and felt and written by writers of different cultures, languages, experiences, classes, and races."
- Find yourself a *"communidad of the word."* Write powerfully about your Chicano culture in such a way that you will "widen and enrich the existing canon" of what constitutes acceptable scholarship in the university. You "have a right and responsibility to do this." And I, and others who are allies, will be here to support you—mightily.[11]

Writing Is Writing: Starting, Sustaining, and Finishing

And, so, dear readers, we have reached the end of my book on scholarly personal narrative writing. I was watching a panel of African-American women writers on C-Span recently. All of them at one time or another had won a prestigious award for their work. Each was witty, wise, and wonderful, and I enjoyed them tremendously. But it was only when I heard a woman whose name I cannot remember say the following that I nodded in vigorous agreement: "Reflection is not writing. Research is not writing. Note taking is not writing. Talking about writing is not writing. Reading is not writing. Reading about writing is not writing. Planning for writing is not writing. Writing is writing. Hear me say this again: *Writing is writing.*"

Granted that all of the assertions preceding her last two are important preconditions for doing scholarly personal narrative writing, it is her final assertion that is most crucial. Writing is writing, period. There is no other way around this. What I've been doing in this book is "writing *about* writing." Is this writing, or is it preparation for writing? For me, the author, I consider my book to be the truest form of writing, because I was able to tell my own story while writing about writing. But *for you,* my readers, this is not writing. It may be a preparation or a motivation for you to start writing. It may be an inspiration, even a provocation. But it isn't writing unless and until you decide to do your own. And this will take perspiration.

In the fall, I will walk into a seminar room with a full house. Fifteen or more graduate students, with 15 or more sets of different needs, talents, and temperaments, will be staring at me, ready to go. All of these students preregistered very early in order to get into my course, and they will be eager at our first meeting for me to psych them up for writing scholarly personal narratives. I will see many familiar faces sitting before me, because I request a personal interview with students who want to enroll for my course. They know what they are getting into beforehand, but they will never really know until they have spent a long semester with me.

A few of these students will never really get started on writing any kind of an extended manuscript, even though they might have the best intentions to do so. It will be false start after false start. The SPN project, for a variety of reasons, will seem much too daunting to them. A few students will be unable to sustain the effort once started, regardless of the intensity of their initial commitment. They will run out of gas, or motivation, or they will just run out of ideas or self-discipline. A few students will almost finish, but not quite. Even though the end is near for these students, it seems a million miles away. As any good salesperson knows, unless you can close the deal, you've got no deal, no matter how great you were leading up to the day of closure. And these students will feel terrible about not closing.

But there will be several students in my seminar who will start, sustain, and close. They will successfully complete an SPN manuscript and be no less for the wear and tear incurred in accomplishing this task. In fact, many will feel transformed in both small and large ways. Listen to some random, postcourse comments from those who finished an SPN. Every single one of them possesses generous amounts of passion, resilience, and faith, qualities that I talked about at the beginning of this chapter as being essential for writing an SPN. This is apparent in the following statements:

- "For the first time, I was able to write openly about my abortion. In the past, the events in my real life were omitted from the academic discourse. And, yet, because of them, they fueled it all! . . . I have decided to keep most of the scary sections in because they are the dark edge of my life . . . and experience suggests that in the light, things resolve! And that when there is space for one's full voice—to speak the whole picture, not just the intellectually abstract one—then I find myself more internally at peace."
- "The whole process of the 50-page paper seemed daunting. But as I have learned time and time again I need to take it one step at a time. . . . I feel that I have written the best paper of my life. . . . There are no words to express how proud I am of myself at accomplishing something I did not think I could do. Digging deeply—the personal—and tying in

quotations from the books we read—the scholarly—was at times very draining, but I pushed on."

• "I still feel more comfortable writing from a slightly more detached perspective. I feel more useful as a spectator—though admittedly as vulnerable sometimes. I used to think that relying too heavily on my own internal conflicts took away from my writing, or my intended message. I've come now to see it as an enhancing quality. Personal narrative is powerful, it's upsetting, and it might even be offending. But no one can argue that it is not genuine. It is the story of one human being, and being that each of us is human, it can be a story about any single one of us."

• "The experience of writing my scholarly personal narrative was deeply felt at every level—spiritually, emotionally, mentally, and physically. . . . Oh, at times it was maddening and sad and exhilarating, and I couldn't fall asleep at night because my brain was racing with ideas. But I loved the genre and particularly the personal self-examination. I was able to dive deep and resurface with a clearer sense of my truths. This kind of writing may be a tough act to follow."

• "I listened to my classmates publicly giving voice to themselves as they read aloud their SPNs about their losses, their despair. But at the same time, I heard them wrestle humor out of pain and scrape at some emotional scar tissue. We all crafted our lives into possibilities, hope, and beginnings. We started the healing that we began with the telling. We gave voice to something never before named. We brought the dark to new light. We uncovered something that for too long lay in the shadows. . . . And yet the telling of our stories had a worth and a certain meaning beyond ourselves. We got glimpses of the universal . . . our stories were scholarly in that they were always in service of an idea, full of vulnerability and yet full of conviction. By lacing our personal stories with allusions to scholarly texts, thin stories became thick for others who have walked these same intellectual paths. We now had stories that resonated with our heads as well as with our hearts."

• "I started this course as a skeptic. I was afraid that if I chose to do an SPN, it would not be seen as a 'real' dissertation by the academy, much less by my friends outside the academy who would wonder what the hell I was doing. Yet the more I learned about SPN, the more I was attracted to the stories, for it is the stories that helped me become the LGBT [lesbian, gay, bisexual, and transgendered] ally that I am today. Without story, I do not think I would be moved to action. . . . What has been particularly valuable is thinking of myself as the research subject. If I went out and interviewed other allies, I would be the middlewoman, taking their experiences and writing about them with my subjective lens.

Writing about myself and my own experience seems much more authentic and true. . . . All of my research questions can be used on myself, so why not use them this way?"

And finally, I leave the last comment on personal narrative writing to my favorite writer on writing, Anne Lamott:

> My students ask, "so why does our writing matter?" Because of the spirit I say. Because of the heart. Writing and reading decrease our sense of isolation. They deepen and widen and expand our sense of life; they feed the soul. When writers make us shake our heads with the exactness of their prose and their truths, and even make us laugh about ourselves or life, our buoyancy is restored. We are given a shot at dancing with, or at least clapping along with, the absurdity of life, instead of being squashed by it over and over again. . . . Even if you never publish a word, you have something important to pour yourself into."[12]

Notes

Chapter 1

1. See Bruner, *Acts of Meaning*, 12. Bruner has helped me to see that "universalizability" need have nothing whatever to do with Kant's categorical principle of moral universalizability, which postmodernists have called "just another metaphysical rule of judgment," somewhat like the Golden Rule. This principle might be useful some of the time for some people but not all of the time for all people. Neither does universalizability have to carry the verifiability burden of scientific truth: something is universalizable only to the extent that it is duplicable, confirmable, predictable, and measurable. Rather, universalizability as a criterion of SPN truth has much more to do with applicability, extension, commonality, consensus, and relevance; or what I sometimes call "narrative overlap." Is there anything in someone else's story that overlaps or coincides with my own, or with others' stories? To the extent that there is, then I would argue that an SPN has universalizable value. There is nothing metaphysical or scientific in this truth claim of mine. I happen to believe, along with Jung, although I can't prove it beyond a shadow of a doubt to metaphysicians and scientists, that all our stories contain at least some seeds of universal appeal. Certainly they have something to teach all of us at some level. Thus, for me, a good SPN is both particular and universal in its appeal. Also, see two recent works that discuss narrative writing in the humanities as a scholarly genre with its own truth criteria: Haroian-Guerin, ed., *The Personal Narrative*; Holdstein and Bleich, eds., *Personal Effects*. Also, see an earlier work that stresses dialogue and caring as major truth criteria for narrative writing in education: Witherell and Noddings, eds., *Stories Lives Tell*.

2. See, perhaps, the major statement on the ever-changing scientific paradigm: Kuhn, *The Structure of Scientific Revolutions*. Also, see Feyerabend, *Against Method*.

3. One such text is by the Pulitzer Prize winner Richard Rhodes: *How to Write*. A more popularized work, but just as useful, is Lamott's *Bird by Bird*.

4. I include in this category books like the immensely popular *The Craft of Research*, by Booth, Columb, and Williams. This practical guide to doing research, while very useful to writers who are working on more conventional term papers,

theses, and dissertations, has nothing whatever to say about crafting a work of personal narrative scholarship.

5. Postmodernism is a complex and slippery term, almost impossible to pin down. I use it here mainly as a way to describe a particular perspective on the meaning of truth. "Meaning" is a word I prefer to "truth." The world may, indeed, exist outside of us, but the truth resides *inside* us, shaped ineluctably by our temperaments, human languages, personal and social narratives, and formative communities of belonging and socialization. Our personal stories of meaning are potentially infinite in number. So, too, therefore, are our truth criteria. See Rorty, *Contingency, Irony, and Solidarity*. Also, see Ives, "The Whole Truth," 275.

6. A wonderful argument by a highly respected scholar in support of the work of public intellectuals is developed by Gerald Graff, *Clueless in Academe*. Also, see Jacoby, *The Last Intellectuals*. For a critique of the idea of "public intellectual," see Fish, *Professional Correctness*, 115–126.

7. See, for example, Kirsch, *Women Writing the Academy*; Welch, Latterell, Moore, and Carter-Tod, eds., *The Dissertation and The Discipline*.

8. Rorty, *Contingency, Irony, and Solidarity*, 3–20.

9. See John W. Creswell, *Qualitative Inquiry and Research Design*. Creswell identifies five ways of doing qualitative research: biography, phenomenology, grounded theory, ethnography, and case study. In my opinion, the five approaches could work for SPN writers, *as long as the subject being studied is the researcher-scholar-writer* and not the ethnographic "other." What I dislike about referring to SPN as just another type of qualitative study is that SPN is a scholarly methodology that stands on its own as a genre, beyond any need to conflate it with an ethnographic approach. While it has some things in common with qualitative research, its differences are far greater than its similarities. For starters, the self of the writer-scholar-researcher is always the central pivot for SPN study. Other selves get introduced into the SPN narrative mainly as useful tools for exploring the writer's narrative, as well as for examining the more universal themes inherent in the writer's narrative. Having said this, I must mention one recent effort by a "qualitative/cultural autobiographical scholar" encouraging researchers to write themselves into their research: Rhoads, "Traversing the Great Divide." Alas, however, even though the American Educational Research Association is getting into the alternative dissertation act, albeit with great caution, it still starts with the premise that empirically based, scientific research is best. See, for example, Duke and Beck, "Education Should Consider Alternative Formats for the Dissertation."

10. Jerome Bruner, *Acts of Meaning*, 111–112. See also Bruner's *The Culture of Education*. His chapter in this latter book on "The Narrative Construal of Reality" is one of the most penetrating arguments I've seen for the need to know people's stories in order to know what makes them tick. Bruner also argues in this book (p. 13) that "stories about reality," no matter how idiosyncratic, always contain universal elements. These are what bind people together "for a life in culture," Finally, Bruner argues that "self-making is always the product of self-telling" in his latest book, *Making Stories*, 99.

Chapter 2

1. All the quotations are taken from Haroian-Guerin, ed., *The Personal Narrative*, 14, 17–18, 33, 130, 215.
2. Lamott, *Bird by Bird*, 201.
3. Gornick, *The Situation and the Story*, 91.
4. Smith, "Make Me a Letter," 43–62. Also, see Goodson, ed., *Studying Teachers' Lives*, for an overview of a number of research methodologies for studying teachers' lives, particularly autobiographical approaches.
5. Gillett and Beer, eds. *Our Own Agendas*, xvi.
6. Holdstein and Bleich, eds., *Personal Effects*, 1.
7. Nash, *Spirituality, Ethics, Religion, and Teaching*.
8. These aphorisms are adapted from my *Spirituality, Ethics, Religion, and Teaching*, 202–204.
9. The notion that truth has no bottom, no final line that is beyond further interpretation; that it is interpretation, not truth, that goes "all the way down," is Stanley Fish's. For example, see his *The Trouble with Principle*.
10. For a thorough and readable history of changes in the field of literary studies, see Graff, *Professing Literature*. For a bracing critique of these changes, see Goodheart, *The Skeptic Disposition*. For a very scholarly explanation and defense of a narrative approach to literary studies, see Abbot, *The Cambridge Introduction to Narrative*.
11. The classic statement of how much the social sciences have changed methodologically, particularly anthropology, is Geertz, *Local Knowledge*; see especially his essay "Blurred Genres: The Refiguration of Social Thought," 19–35. For a more moderate statement about how conceptions of scientific knowledge have changed throughout the 20th century, see Kitcher, *Science, Truth, and Democracy*. For a traditional defense of a view of science and reason, based on the posit of a series of objective principles that are independent of particular cultures and personal points of view, see Nagel, *The Last Word*. I myself find important, overlapping narrative meanings in all three books, and I wouldn't hesitate to assign all of them as important historical background for a course on scholarly personal narrative writing.
12. All my quotations and comments about Ruth Behar come mainly from my reading of *The Vulnerable Observer*, 13, 31, 33, 161–167; also, see her *Translated Woman*. For a wonderful collection of essays that touch directly on much that I am saying about SPNs, see *Women Writing Culture*, edited by Ruth Behar and Deborah A. Gordon.
13. Behar, *The Vulnerable Observer*, 33.

Chapter 3

1. Rhodes, *How to Write*, 2.
2. In Bender, *Writing Personal Essays*, n.p.
3. See Nash, *Religious Pluralism in the Academy*.

4. Rhodes, *How to Write*, 3.
5. See Zinsser, *On Writing Well*.
6. Divakaruni, "New Insights into the Novel?" 40–41.
7. McCullough, "Climbing into Another Head," 163. Also, see Egan, *Teaching as Story Telling*, for a pedagogical application of McCullough's insight about the universal appeal of stories. According to Egan, a narrative approach to teaching subject matter has the potential to cover the entire curriculum, including such disciplines as social studies, language arts, mathematics, and science.
8. Dillard, *The Writing Life*, 78.
9. Ibid., 58–59.
10. Atwood, *Negotiating with the Dead*, xix.
11. Strunk and White, *The Elements of Style*, 79.
12. Keyes, *The Courage to Write*, 99–113.
13. Rorty, *Contingency, Irony, and Solidarity*, 152.
14. All the quotations in this section are taken from Tompkins, *A Life in School*, 76, 95, 12, 200.

Chapter 4

1. Aronie, *Writing from the Heart*, 164.
2. Solomon, *The Passions*, 405.
3. Tompkins, *A Life in School*, 227.
4. Tillich, *The Courage to Be*, 1, 17, 37, 181.
5. Frankl, *Man's Search for Meaning*, 186.

Chapter 5

1. For a fine SPN on the subject of vocation, see Palmer, *Let Your Life Speak*.
2. Handelman, "Knowledge Has a Face," 142.
3. Cited by Handelman, ibid., 121.
4. Edmundson, *Teacher*, 13.
5. Nash, *Spirituality, Ethics, Religion, and Teaching*, 212.
6. Many of these questions are raised in a biting, Marxist critique of postmodernism by Eagleton, *The Illusions of Postmodernism*. I recommend this book highly to both advocates and critics of postmodernism. I also strongly recommend a book for both groups that contains a number of excellent essays by supporters of postmodernism: Anderson ed., *The Truth about the Truth*.
7. Goldberg, *Writing Down the Bones*, 14.
8. See a probing philosophical discussion on these themes in what I think is Palmer's best book, *To Know as We Are Known*.

Chapter 6

1. Eakin, *How Our Lives Become Stories*. See also Couser, *Vulnerable Subjects*.
2. See Nash, *"Real World" Ethics*.

3. Patai, "Ethical Problems of Personal Narratives, or Who Should Eat the Last Piece of Cake?", 5.

4. Baker, "Life with Mother," 37.

5. Nash, *Spirituality, Ethics, Religion, and Teaching,* 25–28.

6. Quoted in Ives, "The Whole Truth," 273.

7. Kopp, *If You Meet the Buddha on the Road, Kill Him!*

8. Aronie, *Writing from the Heart,* 63.

9. Glenn, "Look Who's Teaching," D2.

10. See Villanueva, "Cuentos De Mi Historia," 276.

11. Alvarez, "On Finding a Latino Voice," 126–133.

12. Lamott, *Bird by Bird,* 236–237.

Bibliography

Abbot, H. Porter. *The Cambridge Introduction to Narrative*. New York: Cambridge University Press, 2002.

Alvarez, Julia. "On Finding a Latino Voice." In *The Writing Life: Writers on How They Think and Work*, edited by Maria Arana. New York: Public Affairs, 2003.

Anderson, Walter Truett, ed. *The Truth about the Truth: De-confusing and Reconstructing the Postmodern World*. New York: Tarcher/Putnam, 1995.

Aronie, Nancy Slonim. *Writing from the Heart: Tapping the Power of Your Inner Voice*. New York: Hyperion, 1998.

Atwood, Margaret. *Negotiating with the Dead: A Writer on Writing*. New York: Cambridge University Press, 2002.

Baker, Russell. "Life with Mother." In *Inventing the Truth: The Art and Craft of Memoir*, edited by William Zinsser. Boston: Houghton Mifflin, 1998.

Barber, Red. *Show Me the Way to Go Home*. Philadelphia: Westminster Press, 1971.

Behar, Ruth. *Translated Woman: Crossing the Border with Esperanza's Story*. Boston: Beacon Press, 1993.

———. *The Vulnerable Observer: Anthropology That Breaks Your Heart*. Boston: Beacon Press, 1996.

Behar, Ruth, and Deborah A. Gordon, eds. *Women Writing Culture*. Berkeley: University of California Press, 1995.

Bender Shelia. *Writing Personal Essays: How to Shape Your Life Experience for the Page*. Cincinnati, OH: Writer's Digest Books, 1995.

Booth, Wayne C., Gregory G. Columb, and Joseph M. Williams. *The Craft of Research*. Chicago: University of Chicago Press, 1995.

Bruner, Jerome. *The Process of Education*. Cambridge, MA: Harvard University Press, 1977.

———. *Acts of Meaning*. Cambridge, MA: Harvard University Press, 1990.

———. *The Culture of Education*. Cambridge, MA: Harvard University Press, 1996.

———. *Making Stories: Law, Literature, Life*. New York: Farrar, Strauss, and Giroux, 2002.

Couser, Thomas G. *Vulnerable Subjects: Ethics and Life Writing*. Ithaca, NY: Cornell University Press, 2004.

Creswell, John W. *Qualitative Inquiry and Research Design: Choosing among Five Traditions.* Thousand Oaks, CA: Sage Publications, 1998.

Dillard, Annie. *The Writing Life.* New York: HarperPerennial, 1990.

Divakaruni, Chitra. "New Insights into the Novel? Try Reading Three Hundred." In *Writers on Writing.* New York: Times Books, 2003.

Duke, Nell K., and Sarah W. Beck. "Education Should Consider Alternative Formats for the Dissertation." *Educational Researcher* (April 1999): 31–36.

Eagleton, Terry. *The Illusions of Postmodernism.* Cambridge, UK: Blackwell, 1996.

Eakin, John Paul. *How Our Lives Become Stories: Making Selves.* New York: Cornell University Press, 1995.

Edelman, Marian Wright. *Lanterns: A Memoir of Mentors.* Boston: Beacon Press, 1999.

Edmundson, Mark. *Teacher.* New York: Random House, 2002.

Egan, Kieran. *Teaching as Story Telling: An Alternative Approach to Teaching and Curriculum in the Elementary School.* Chicago: University of Chicago Press, 1986.

Feyerabend, Paul. *Against Method.* New York: Schocken Books, 1977.

Fish, Stanley, *Professional Correctness: Literary Studies and Political Change.* New York: Oxford University Press, 1995.

_____. *The Trouble with Principle.* Cambridge, MA: Harvard University Press, 1999.

Frankl, Viktor Emil. *Man's Search for Meaning: An Introduction to Logotherapy.* Boston: Beacon Press, 1992.

Geertz, Clifford. *Local Knowledge: Further Essays in Interpretive Anthropology.* New York: Basic Books, 1983.

Gillet, Margaret, and Ann Beer, eds. *Our Own Agendas: Autobiographical Essays by Women.* Montreal: McGill-Queen's University Press, 1995.

Glenn, Joshua. "Look Who's Teaching." *Boston Sunday Globe,* August 17, 2003, D2.

Goldberg, Natalie. *Writing Down the Bones: Freeing the Writer.* Boston: Shamhala, 1986.

Goodheart, Eugene. *The Skeptic Disposition: Deconstruction, Ideology, and Other Matters.* Princeton, NJ: Princeton University Press, 1984.

Goodson, Ivor, F., ed. *Studying Teachers' Lives.* New York: Teachers College Press, 1992.

Gornick, Vivian. *The Situation and the Story: The Art of Personal Narrative.* New York: Farrar, Strauss, and Giroux, 2001.

Graff, Gerald. *Professing Literature: An Institutional History.* Chicago: University of Chicago Press, 1987.

_____. *Clueless in Academe: How Schooling Obscures the Life of the Mind.* New Haven, CT: Yale University Press, 2003.

Handelman, Susan. "Knowledge Has a Face: The Jewish, the Personal, and the Pedagogical," in *Personal Effects: The Social Character of Scholarly Writing,* edited by Deborah H. Holdstein and David Bleich. Logan, UT: Utah State University Press, 2001.

Haroian-Guerin, Gil, ed. *The Personal Narrative: Writing Ourselves as Teachers and Scholars*. Portland, ME: Calendar Islands Publishers, 1999.

Holdstein, Deborah H., and David Bleich, ed., *Personal Effects: The Social Character of Scholarly Writing*. Logan, UT: Utah State University Press, 2001.

Ives, Peter M. "The Whole Truth," in *The Fourth Genre: Contemporary Writers of/ on Creative Nonfiction*, 2nd ed., edited by Robert L. Root and Michael Steinberg. New York: Longman, 2002.

Jacoby, Russell. *The Last Intellectuals: American Culture in the Age of Academe*. New York: Basic Books, 2000.

Keyes, Ralph. *The Courage to Write: How Writers Transcend Fear*. New York: Henry Holt, 1995.

Kirsch, Gesa E. *Women Writing the Academy: Audience, Authority, and Transformation*. Carbondale, IL: Southern Illinois University Press, 1993.

Kitcher, Philip. *Science, Truth, and Democracy*. New York: Oxford University Press, 2001.

Kopp, Sheldon B. *If You Meet the Buddha on the Road, Kill Him!* New York: Bantam, 1976.

Kuhn, Thomas S. *The Structure of Scientific Revolutions*. Chicago: University of Chicago Press, 1970.

Lamott, Anne. *Bird by Bird: Some Instructions on Writing and Life*. New York: Pantheon, 1994.

McCullough, David. "Climbing into Another Head." In *The Writing Life: Writers on How They Think and Work*, edited by Marie Arana. New York: Public Affairs, 2003.

Nagel, Thomas. *The Last Word*. New York: Oxford University Press, 1997.

Nash, Robert J. *Religious Pluralism in the Academy: Opening the Dialogue*. New York: Peter Lang, 2001.

_____. *"Real World" Ethics: Frameworks for Educators and Human Service Professionals*. 2nd ed. New York: Teachers College Press, 2002.

_____. *Spirituality, Ethics, Religion, and Teaching: A Professor's Journey*. New York: Peter Lang, 2002.

Palmer, Parker J. *To Know as We Are Known: A Spirituality of Education*. New York: HarperCollins, 1983.

_____. *Let Your Life Speak: Listening for the Voice of Vocation*. San Francisco, CA: Jossey-Bass, 2000.

Patai, Daphne. "Ethical Problems of Personal Narratives, or Who Should Eat the Last Piece of Cake?" *International Journal of Oral History* 8 (1987): 5–27.

Phillips, Christopher. *Socrates Café: A Fresh Taste of Philosopy*. New York: W.W. Norton, 2001.

Rhoads, Robert A. "Traversing the Great Divide: Writing the Self into Qualitative Research and Narrative." *Studies in Symbolic Interaction* 26 (2003): 235–259.

Rhodes, Richard. *How to Write: Advice and Reflections*. New York: William Morrow, 1995.

Rorty, Richard. *Contingency, Irony, and Solidarity*. Cambridge, UK: Cambridge University Press, 1989.

————. *Philosophy and Social Hope*. New York: Penguin, 1999.

Smith, Louise Z. "Make Me a Letter." In *The Personal Narrative: Writing Ourselves as Teachers and Scholars*, edited by Gil Haroian-Guerin. Portland, ME: Calendar Islands, 1999.

Solomon, Robert. *The Passions*. Notre Dame, IN: University of Notre Dame Press, 1983.

Tillich, Paul. *The Courage to Be*. New Haven: Yale University Press, 1952.

Tompkins, Jane. *A Life in School: What the Teacher Learned*. New York: Addison-Wesley, 1996.

Villanueva, Victor. "Cuentos De Mi Historia." In *Personal Effects: The Social Character of Scholarly Writing*, edited by Deborah H. Holdstein and David Bleich. Logan, UT: Utah State University Press, 2001.

Welch, Nancy, Catherine G. Latterell, Cindy Moore, and Sheila Carter-Tod, eds. *The Dissertation and the Discipline: Reinventing Composition Studies*. Portsmouth, NH: Boynton/Cook, 2002.

Witherell, Carol, and Nel Noddings, eds. *Stories Lives Tell: Narrative and Dialogue in Education*. New York: Teachers College Press, 1991.

Zinsser, William. ed., *On Writing Well: The Classic Guide to Writing Nonfiction*. New York: Quill, 2001.

Recommended Books
on Writing

I list here several books on writing and usage, most that I have not cited in the text itself. I have found each of these texts to be very helpful in writing SPNs. I have used many of them in my writing course, and I recommend them highly.

The American Heritage Book of English Usage: A Practical and Authoritative Guide to Contemporary English. Boston: Houghton Mifflin, 1996.

Chicago Manual of Style, The. 15th ed. Chicago: University of Chicago Press, 2003.

Conroy, Frank, ed. *The Eleventh Draft: Craft and the Writing Life from the Iowa Writers' Workshop.* New York: HarperCollins, 1999.

Dumond, Val. *Grammar for Grownups.* New York: HarperCollins, 1993.

Gerard, Philip. *Creative Nonfiction: Researching and Crafting Stories of Real Life.* Cincinnati, OH: Story Press, 1996.

Gutkind, Lee. *The Art of Creative Nonfiction: Writing and Selling the Literature of Reality.* New York: Wiley, 1997.

King, Stephen. *On Writing: A Memoir of the Craft.* New York: Pocket Books, 2000.

Lamb, Brian. *Booknotes: America's Finest Authors on Reading, Writing, and the Power of Ideas.* New York: Times Books, 1997.

Maisel, Eric. *Deep Writing: 7 Principles That Bring Ideas to Life.* New York: Tarcher/Putnam, 1999.

The Oxford American College Dictionary. New York: G. P. Putnam's Sons, 2002.

Phifer, Nan. *Memoirs of the Soul: Writing Your Spiritual Autobiography.* Cincinnati, OH: Walking Stick Press, 2002.

The Random House Thesaurus: College Edition. New York: Random House, 1990.

Rogers, Bruce Holland. *Word Work: Surviving and Thriving as a Writer.* Montpelier, VT: Invisible Cities Press, 2002.

Roorbach, Bill. *Writing Life Stories.* Cincinnati, OH: Story Press, 1998.

Siegal, Allan M., and William G. Connolly, eds. *The New York Times Manual of Style and Usage*. New York: Times Books, 1999.

Strunk, William Jr., and E. B. White. *The Elements of Style*. 4th ed. New York: Longman, 2000.

Turabian, Kate L. *A Manual for Writers of Term Papers, Theses, and Dissertations*. 6th ed. Chicago: University of Chicago Press, 1996.

Index

Constructs, 57–59, 63, 78, 83, 114–115
Context, in postmodernism, 39–40
Conversational style, 101
Courage encouragement (Nash), 54
Courage to Be, The (Tillich), 91–92
Courage to Write, The (Keyes), 69–70
Couser, Thomas G., 164 n. 1
Craft of writing, 64–65
Creative voice, 57, 71
Creswell, John W., 162 n. 9
Critical literary theory, 45
Critical theory, 150
Cronbach, Lee, 23

Dave (student), 101–107, 126
David (student), 32, 81–85, 97
Dewey, John, 57, 105
Dickey, James, 52, 128
Dillard, Annie, 48, 63, 66–67, 148, 164 n. 8
Dissertations (theses). *See* Scholarly personal narrative (SPN)
Distortion, 138
Divakaruni, Chitra, 61, 164 n. 6
Diversity, 154
Doug (student), 112–119, 127, 128
Duke, Nell K., 162 n. 9
Duke University, 71

Eagleton, Terry, 164 n. 6
Eakin, John Paul, 130, 132, 164 n. 1
Eastwood, Clint, 74
Eck, Diana, 149
Edelman, Marian Wright, 79, 148
Edmundson, Mark, 102, 164 n. 4
Educationists, 15
Egan, Kieran, 164 n. 7
Eliot, T. S., 72
E-mail, 55–56
Emerson, Ralph Waldo, 24, 75
Epigraphs, 80
Epistolary symposia (Smith), 29
Ethical issues, 36–37, 131–136, 154–156
ethical truth, 137–138

honesty, 136
informed consent, 135
privacy rights, 132–136
Ethnic consciousness, 49–50, 145–146
Etymological fallacy (Nash), 46
Existentialism, 82–85, 88, 97

Faith, in doing scholarly personal narrative, 130–131
Fear of writing, 52–56, 73
Feminism, 72, 147
Feyerabend, Paul, 161 n. 2
Fish, Stanley, 72, 162 n. 6, 163 n. 9
Formal background knowledge, 61–62
Framing (Atwood), 67–68
Frankl, Viktor, 95, 164 n. 5
Freedman, Diane P., 99
Freire, Paulo, 105
Fugitive, The (TV program), 34–36

Gates, Henry Louis, Jr., 42, 149
Gates Millennium Foundation, 146
Geertz, Clifford, 163 n. 11
Generality, 59–60, 85–86, 92
Ghosh, Amitav, 149
Gillett, Margaret, 29, 163 n. 5
Gilligan, Carol, 149
Giovanni, Nikki, 149
Giroux, Henry, 151
Glenn, Joshua, 165 n. 9
Glesne, Corinne, 18
Goethe, G. W. F., 56
Goldberg, Natalie, 112, 164 n. 7
Goleman, Daniel, 84
Goodheart, Eugene, 163 n. 10
Goodson, Ivor F., 163 n. 4
Gordon, Deborah A., 163 n. 12
Gornick, Vivian, 23–24, 27–29, 163 n. 3
Gould, Stephen Jay, 42
Graff, Gerald, 162 n. 6, 163 n. 10
Green, Ann E., 25
Growing Up (Baker), 137
Grumet, Madeleine R., 52, 60
Guerilla interdisciplinarian (Behar), 50

About the Author

Robert J. Nash has been a professor in the College of Education and Social Services, University of Vermont, Burlington, for 35 years. He specializes in philosophy of education, ethics, higher education, and religion, spirituality, and education. He holds graduate degrees in English, Theology, Applied Ethics and Liberal Studies, and Educational Philosophy. He holds faculty appointments in teacher education, higher education administration, and interdisciplinary studies in education. He administers the Interdisciplinary Master's Program, and he teaches ethics and philosophy of education courses across three programs in the college, including the doctoral program in Educational Leadership and Policy Studies. He has published more than 100 articles, book chapters, monographs, and essay book reviews in many of the leading journals in education at all levels. He is a member of the editorial board for the *Journal of Religion and Education*, and one of its frequent contributors. Since 1996, he has published six books, several of them national award winners: *"Real World" Ethics: Frameworks for Educators and Human Service Professionals (1st and 2nd editions); Answering the "Virtuecrats": A Moral Conversation on Character Education; Faith, Hype, and Clarity: Teaching about Religion in American Schools and Colleges; Religious Pluralism in the Academy: Opening the Dialogue;* and *Spirituality, Ethics, Religion, and Teaching: A Professor's Journey.* He has done a variety of consultancies throughout the country for a number of human service organizations and colleges and universities. He has also made a series of major presentations at national conferences and at universities on the topics of ethics, character education, religious pluralism, and moral conversation. In 2003, he was named by the University of Vermont an official university scholar in the social sciences and the humanities.